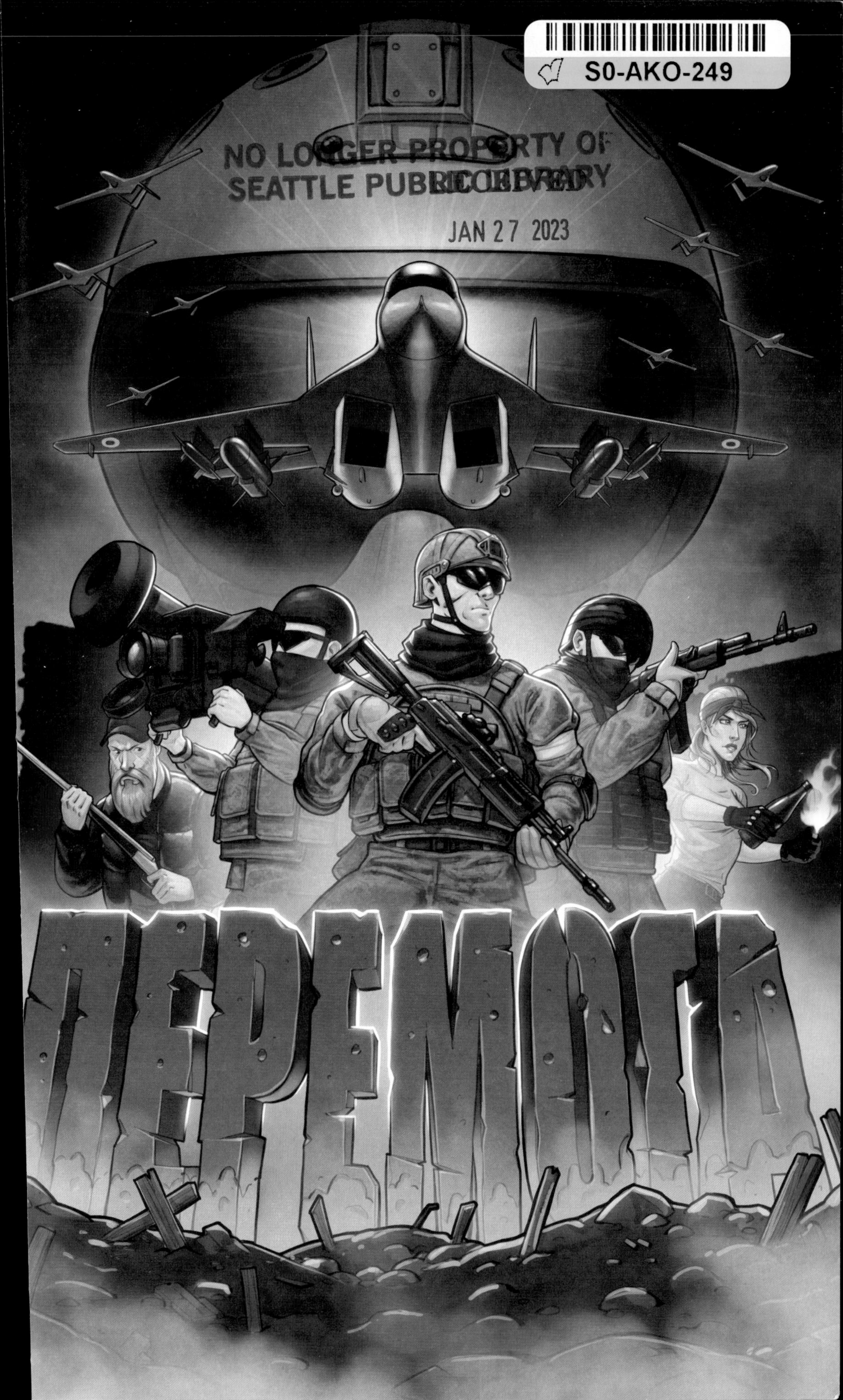
ПЕРЕМОГА

Перемога: Victory for Ukraine

General Producer - Eduard Akhramovych

Project Leader - Viacheslav Buhaiov

Managers - Oleksandr Fylypovych, Olha Vozniuk, Hennadii Shevchenko

Artists - Oleksandr Koreshkov (Episode 1), Kateryna Kosheleva (Episode 2), Yevhenii Tonchylov (Episode 3), Volodymyr Povoroznyk (Episode 4), Ihor Kurilin (Episode 5), Maksym Bohdanovskyi (Episode 6), Bohdana Vitkovska (Episode 7), Nazar Ponik (Episode 8), Kyrylo Malov (Episode 9)

Colors - Oleh Okuniev (Episode 3), Ihor Kurilin (Episode 8)

Cover Artists - Oleksii Bondarenko, Nazar Ponik

Writers - Denys Fadieiev (Episodes 1, 2, 3, 5, 6, 8, 9), Ruslan Samaryk (Episode 4), Bohdana Vitkovska (Episode 7)

Dialogues - Viacheslav Buhaiov (Episodes 5, 8), Denys Fadieiev (Episodes 5, 8)

Interpreter - Hanna Andrieieva

Editor - Becca Grace

Graphic Designer - Sol DeLeo

Marketing Associate - Kae Winters

Digital Marketing Assistant - Kit Burgess

Retouching and Lettering - Vibrraant Publishing Studio

Licensing Specialist - Arika Yanaka

VP of Publishing - Marc Visnick

Editor-in-Chief & Publisher - Stu Levy

A  Manga

TOKYOPOP and ◎ are trademarks or registered trademarks of TOKYOPOP Inc.

TOKYOPOP Inc.
4136 Del Rey Ave., Suite 502
Marina del Rey, CA 90292-5604

E-mail: info@TOKYOPOP.com
Come visit us online at www.TOKYOPOP.com

f www.facebook.com/TOKYOPOP
🐦 www.twitter.com/TOKYOPOP
📷 www.instagram.com/TOKYOPOP

ISBN: 978-1-4278-7322-4

First TOKYOPOP Printing: September 2022
Printed in CANADA

VICTORY FOR UKRAINE

LETTER FROM THE PUBLISHER

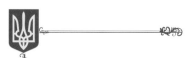

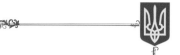

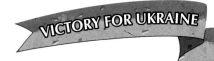

Dear Reader:

It is with a heavy heart that we bring you this publication. War is never a welcome event, but some conflicts are unavoidable and important. Unfortunately, the unprovoked invasion of Ukraine is quite the opposite—it is simply a unilateral act of state violence and greed. The actions of Vladimir Putin and the Russian army have unleashed widespread destruction, atrocity and death and have forced millions of innocent Ukrainians, mainly women and children, to flee their homeland.

Two of those refugees—a young mother, Natalia, and her 3-year-old daughter, Kyra —are living with my family at our home in Berlin, Germany. Following the invasion in February 2022 and soon after the birth of our daughter in March 2022, we attended an event here in Berlin where many Ukrainians – unsure of where to go or what to do next – gathered for fellowship and information. Ukraine's neighbor, Poland, has given refuge to millions of people, with nearly 1 million also now residing in Germany. We have had a wonderful experience with Natalia and little Kyra as two families living as one (my little son Aiden has become Kyra's inseparable bosom buddy), but it breaks my heart to watch her FaceTime every night with her father and grandparents still back in Ukraine. Their neighborhood has been shattered by Russian bombs and last week Natalia's best friend's house was destroyed—the explosion and shrapnel just missing her friend's mother by a dozen yards.

Displacement, anxiety, and fear are now part of daily life for millions of Ukrainians—both at home and abroad. The 9 stories in VICTORY FOR UKRAINE were created entirely by Ukrainians to express their fears, tears, and anger towards "the Enemy." While Ukraine and its people are on the defense, they will never surrender and their resolve and will to fight and rally the world is an inspiration and a shining beacon of freedom.

VICTORY FOR UKRAINE is one way we can not only learn about their struggles but also join them in solidarity. Comics are a truly personal medium and one with unlimited beauty and depth. TOKYOPOP and I are very honored to be able to play a small role in delivering their message to you. Thank you for joining us in welcoming these brave individuals, these creators, these fighters into our homes, and may they one day achieve Перемога: Victory for Ukraine.

Slava Ukraini! – "Glory to Ukraine"

Stu Levy
Publisher, TOKYOPOP

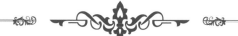

CULTURAL REFERENCES FROM

UKRAINE

This book contains cultural references from Ukraine which you may not be familiar with, so we are including them here. Feel free to refer to this page as you read the stories, or read this in advance so you're prepped before continuing — it's up to you!

AZOVSTAL: The Azovstal Iron and Steel Works became the site of a major battle between Ukraine and Russia during the siege of Mariupol. The plant had bomb shelters and bunkers beneath it, making it a highly defendable position for Ukrainian soldiers. By late April 2022, Azovstal became one of the last strongholds for the Ukrainian defenders. The plant was bombarded by Russia over the course of the battle, and eventually the Ukrainian defenders offered a conditional surrender (see Episode 3).

BRUNO OF QUERFURT: Bruno of Querfurt was a christian missionary bishop and martyr who was beheaded for trying to spread christianity (see pg 61).

DNIEPER RIVER: The Dnieper River is the longest river in Ukraine and the fourth-longest river in Europe. The total length is approx. 1,400 miles (see pg 14).

GHOST OF KYIV: On February 24, 2022, the Russian invasion of Kyiv began. During that first day of the Kyiv offensive, claims began circulating of a pilot who took down several Russian jets alone. That pilot was nicknamed "the Ghost of Kyiv" and became a symbol of hope for the Ukrainian people (see Episode 1).

KHERSON: As a major economic and administrative hub in southern Ukraine, Kherson was the site of aggressive warfare at the start of the Russian invasion of Ukraine. By March 2, 2022, Kherson was reportedly occupied by Russia, leading a majority of Ukrainian citizens to flee. The remaining Ukrainians in the city of Kherson continue to stage protests against Russian occupation (see Episode 8).

KHOKHOLS: A derogatory Russian term for Ukrainians (see pgs 17 & 57).

KONOTOP: Once the site of a war between Ukrainian Cossacks and cavalry units of the Russian tsardom in 1659, Konotop once again became the location of a battle between Ukrainians and Russians in February 2022. Despite the threat of extreme violence should the residents attempt to resist the Russian occupation, the citizens of Konotop refused to surrender (see Episodes 2 and 9).

MARIUPOL: During the siege in February 2022, Russian forces completely bombarded the citizens of Mariupol, leading to near total destruction of residences and thousands of Ukrainian deaths. Both Ukrainian armed forces as well as citizens retreated to the Azovstal Iron and Steel Works until they surrendered in May 2022 (see Episode 3).

MUSCOVITES: Muscovy is an alternative name for the Grand Duchy of Moscow (1263–1547)—the first state in the territory of modern Russia. "Muscovites" were its citizens (see pgs 78-79).

SERPENT'S WALL: Originally built between the 2nd Century BC and 7th Century AD, Serpent's Wall is a system of ancient fortifications. There are several theories as to whom the wall was built by (and when), but all theories revolve around protection against invading nomadic enemies (see Episode 6).

UKROP: A derogatory Russian term for Ukrainians (see pgs 14, 45, 56).

VOLODYMYR THE GREAT: Volodymyr the Great was Grand Prince of Kyiv and ruler of Kievan Rus' from 980 to 1015. Kievan Rus' was a state in eastern and northern Europe from the late 9th to mid-13th Century. He is known for leading the christianization of Kievan Rus' (see pg 61).

ZMIINYI ISLAND: Legend has it that a strong current from the Danube River brought river snakes to the island, which is why the island is called Zmiinyi—Ukrainian for snake (see Episode 5).

EPISODE 1
THE GHOST OF KYIV

ARTIST
OLEKSANDR KORESHKOV

WRITER
DENYS FADIEIEV

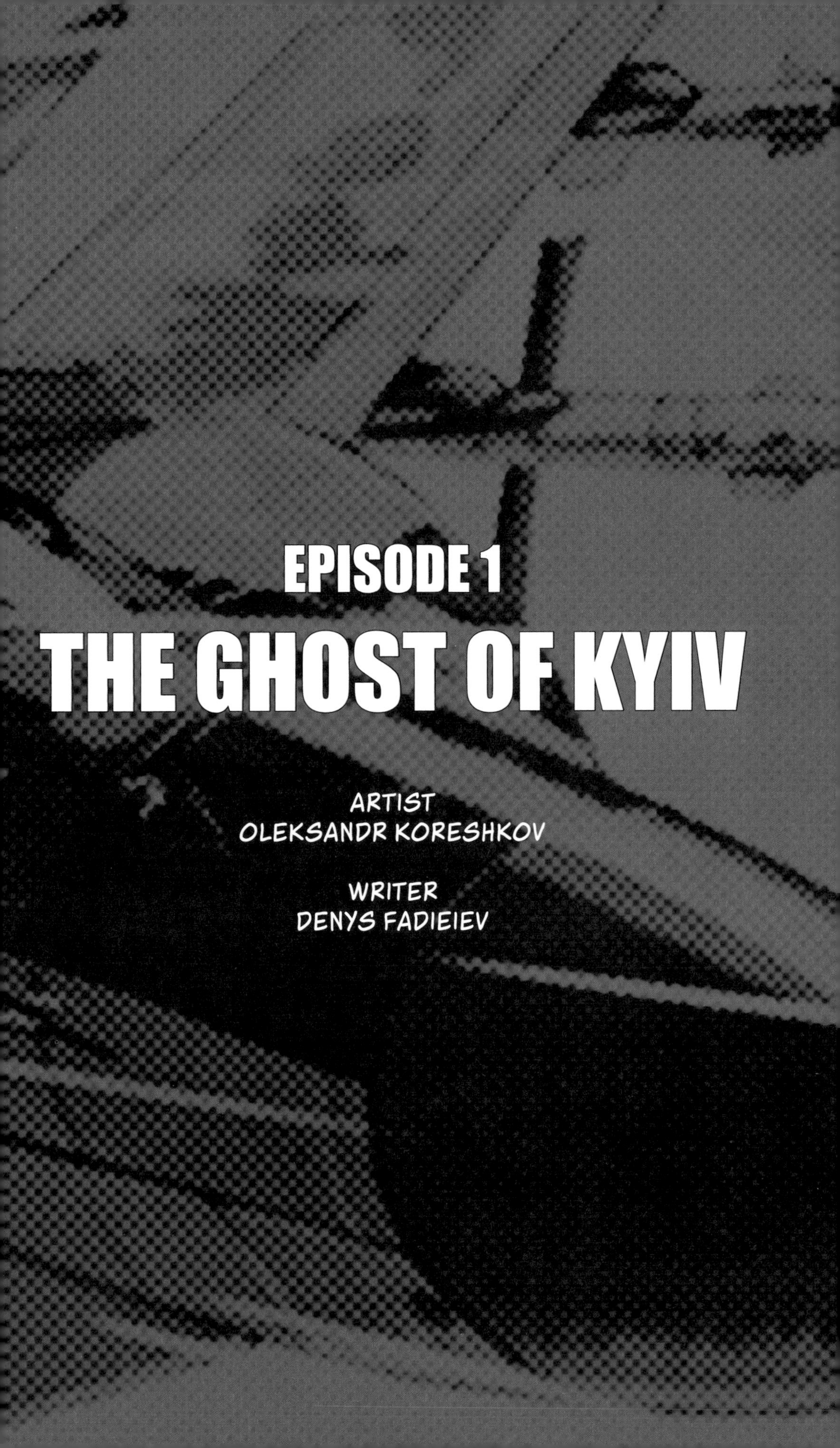

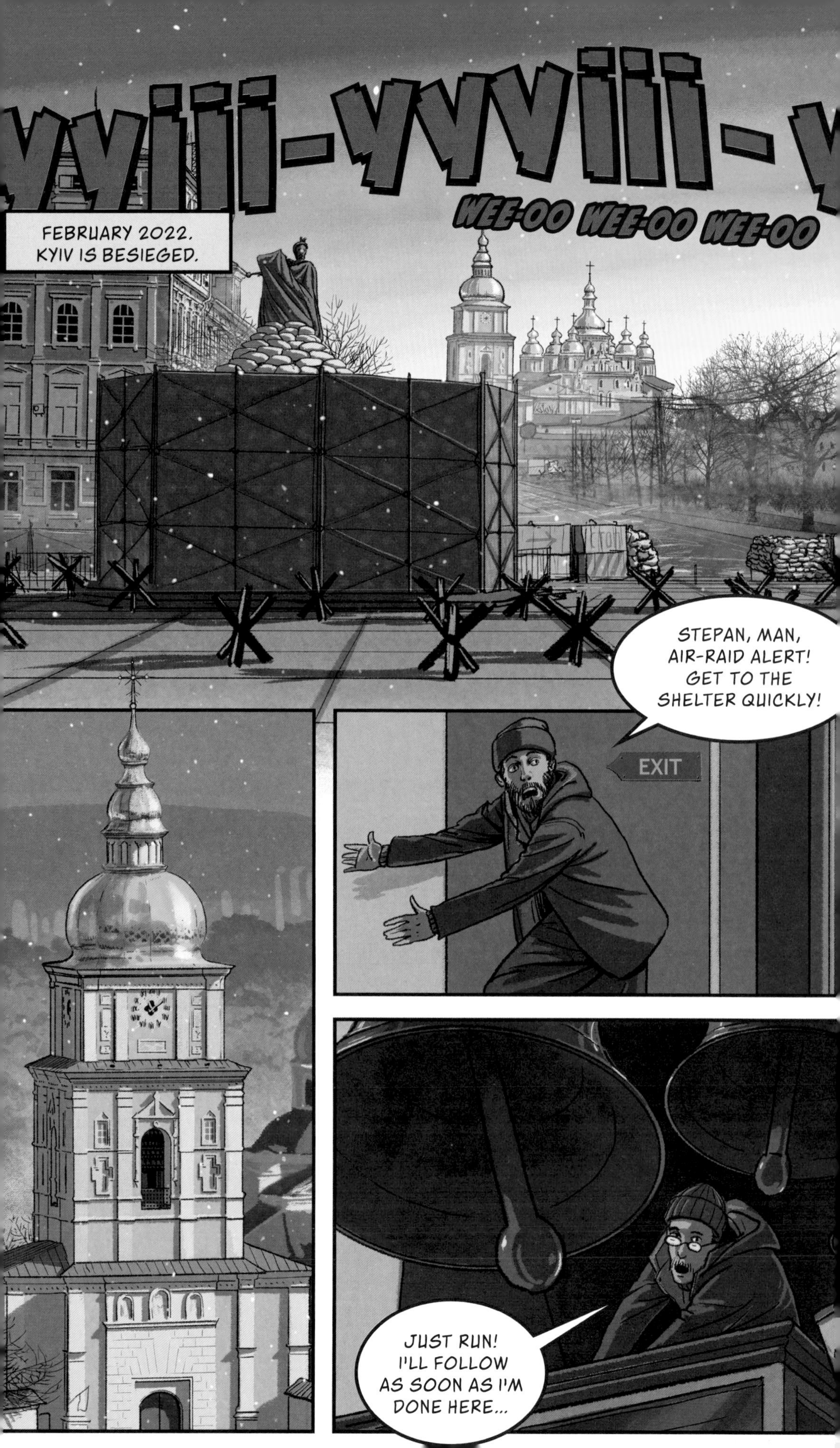
YYIII-YYVIII-Y
WEE-OO WEE-OO WEE-OO
FEBRUARY 2022. KYIV IS BESIEGED.
STEPAN, MAN, AIR-RAID ALERT! GET TO THE SHELTER QUICKLY!
EXIT
JUST RUN! I'LL FOLLOW AS SOON AS I'M DONE HERE...

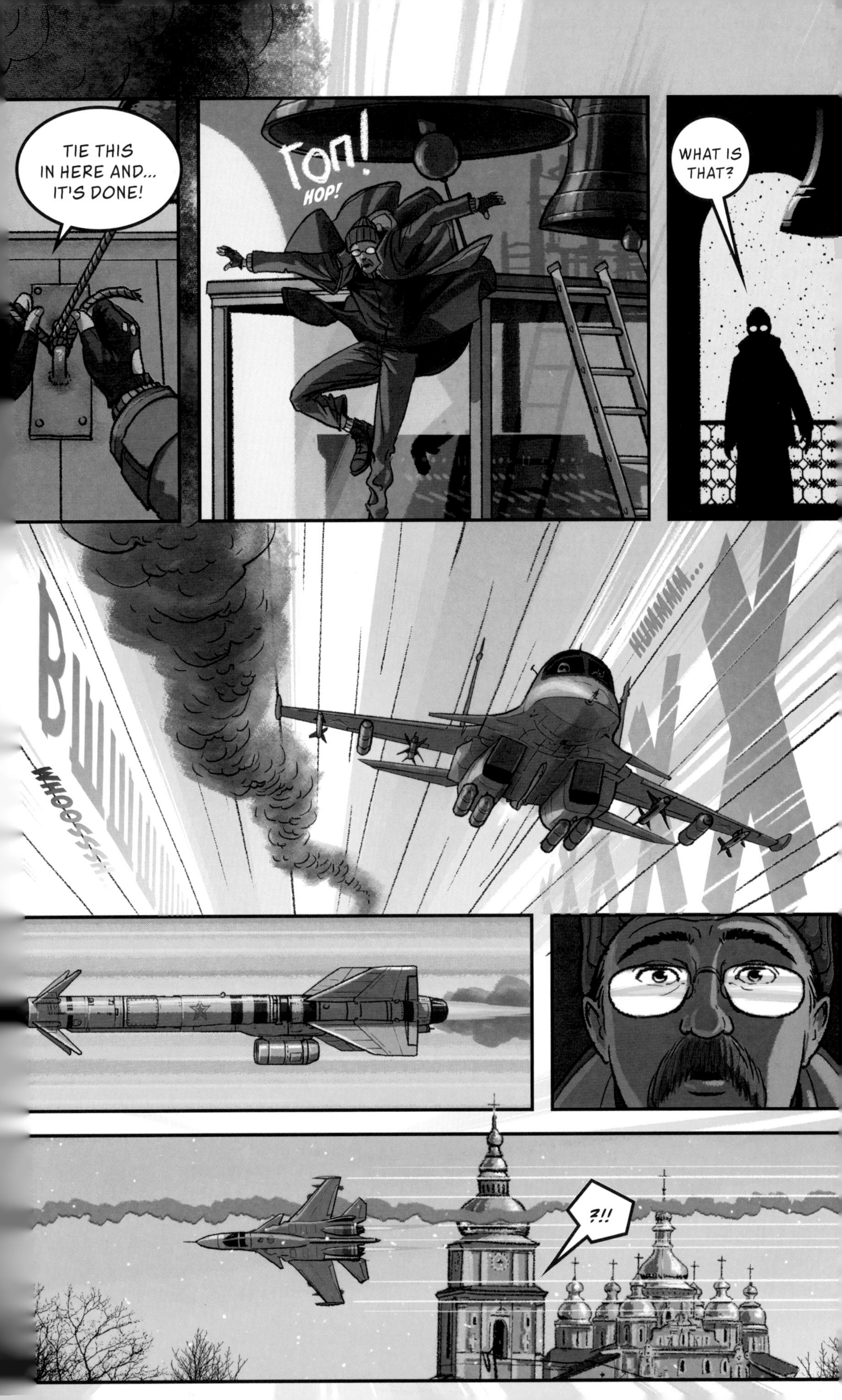
TIE THIS IN HERE AND... IT'S DONE!
ГОП!
HOP!
WHAT IS THAT?
WHOOSSSH..
HUMMMMM...
?!!

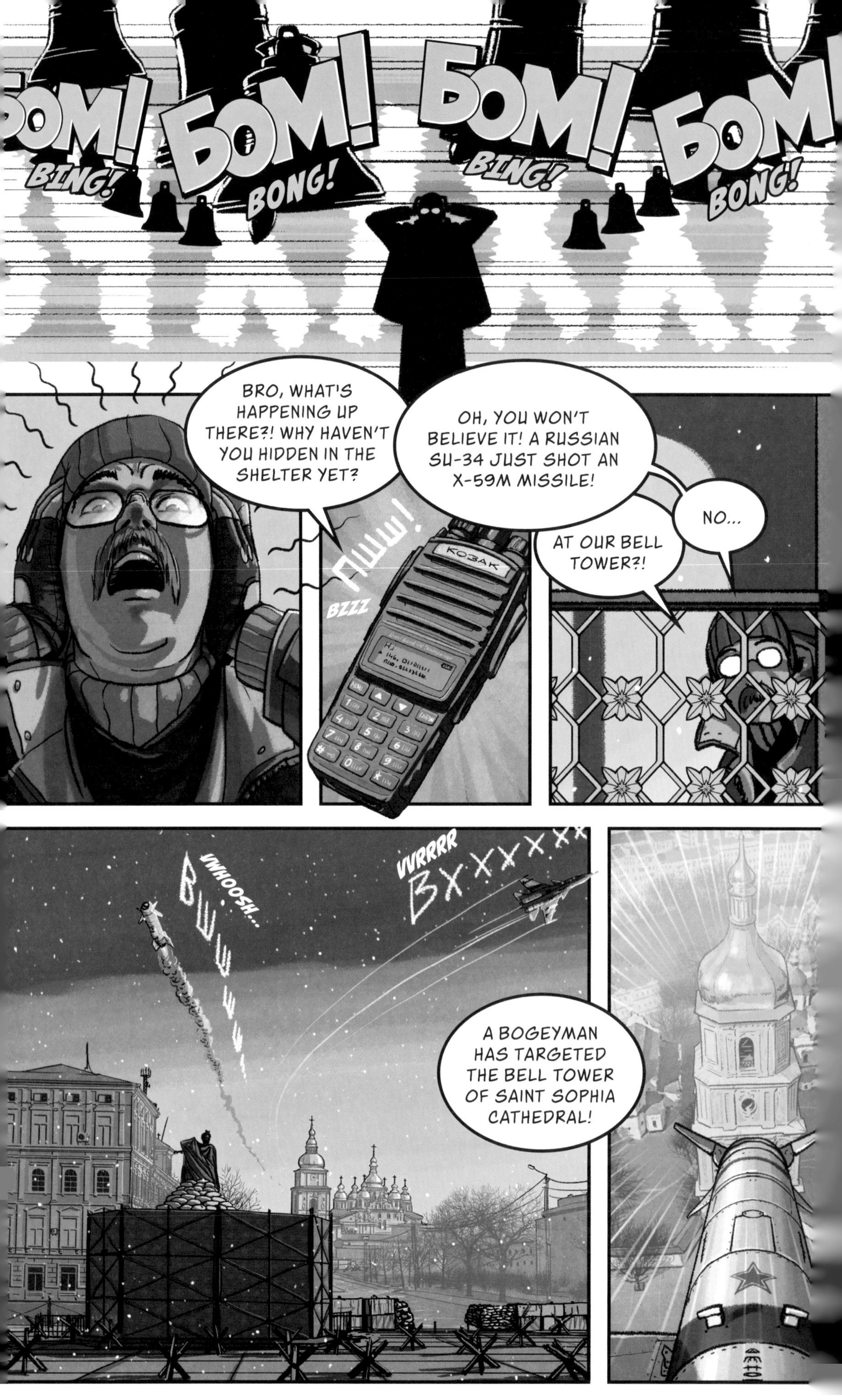
БОМ!
BING!
БОМ!
BONG!
БОМ!
BING!
БОМ
BONG!
BRO, WHAT'S HAPPENING UP THERE?! WHY HAVEN'T YOU HIDDEN IN THE SHELTER YET?
OH, YOU WON'T BELIEVE IT! A RUSSIAN SU-34 JUST SHOT AN X-59M MISSILE!
ПШШ!
BZZZ
КОЗАК
AT OUR BELL TOWER?!
NO...
WHOOSH...
ВШШ
VVRRRR
ВХХХХХ
A BOGEYMAN HAS TARGETED THE BELL TOWER OF SAINT SOPHIA CATHEDRAL!

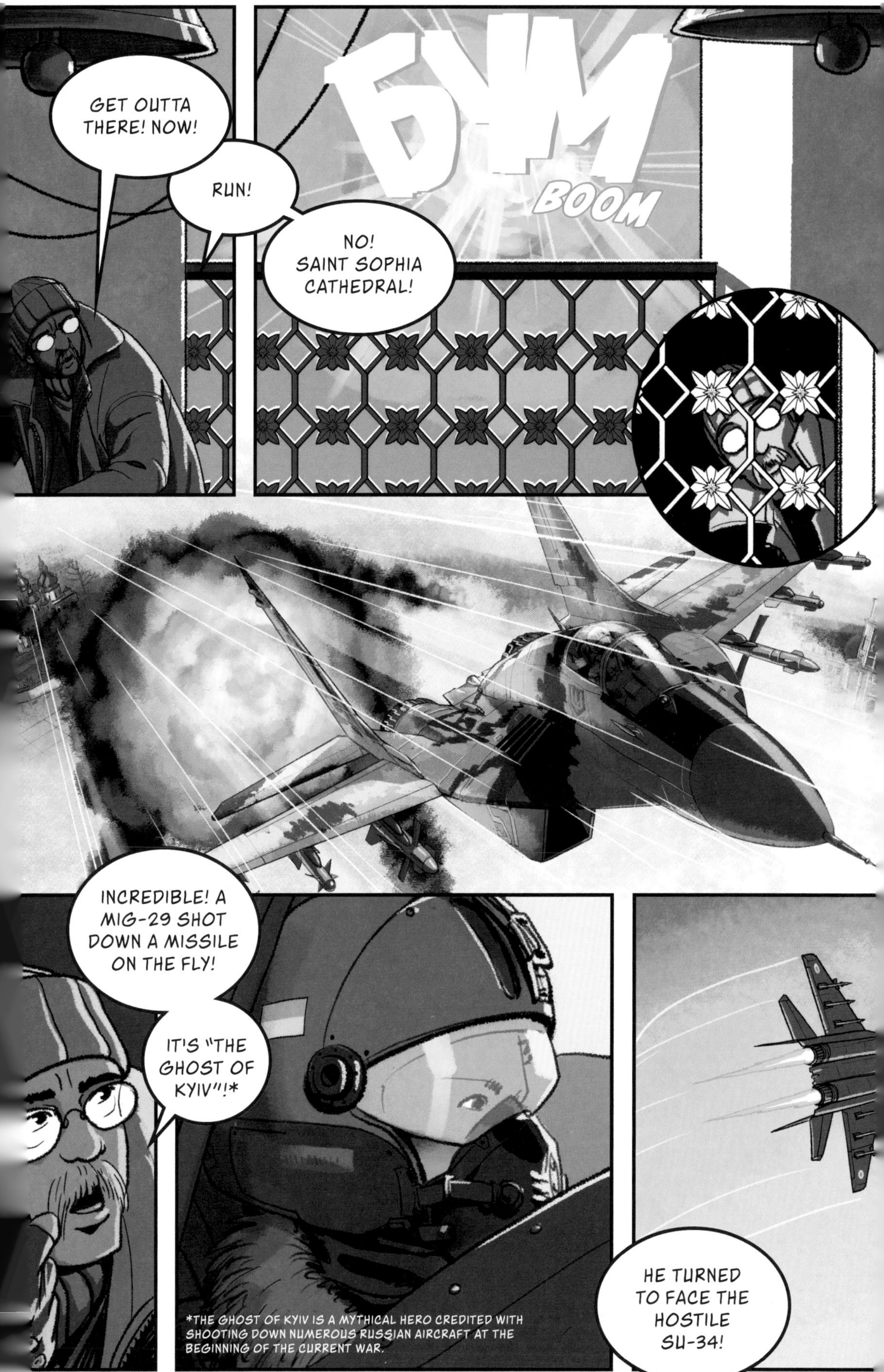
GET OUTTA THERE! NOW!
RUN!
БУМ
BOOM
NO! SAINT SOPHIA CATHEDRAL!
INCREDIBLE! A MIG-29 SHOT DOWN A MISSILE ON THE FLY!
IT'S "THE GHOST OF KYIV"!*
*THE GHOST OF KYIV IS A MYTHICAL HERO CREDITED WITH SHOOTING DOWN NUMEROUS RUSSIAN AIRCRAFT AT THE BEGINNING OF THE CURRENT WAR.
HE TURNED TO FACE THE HOSTILE SU-34!

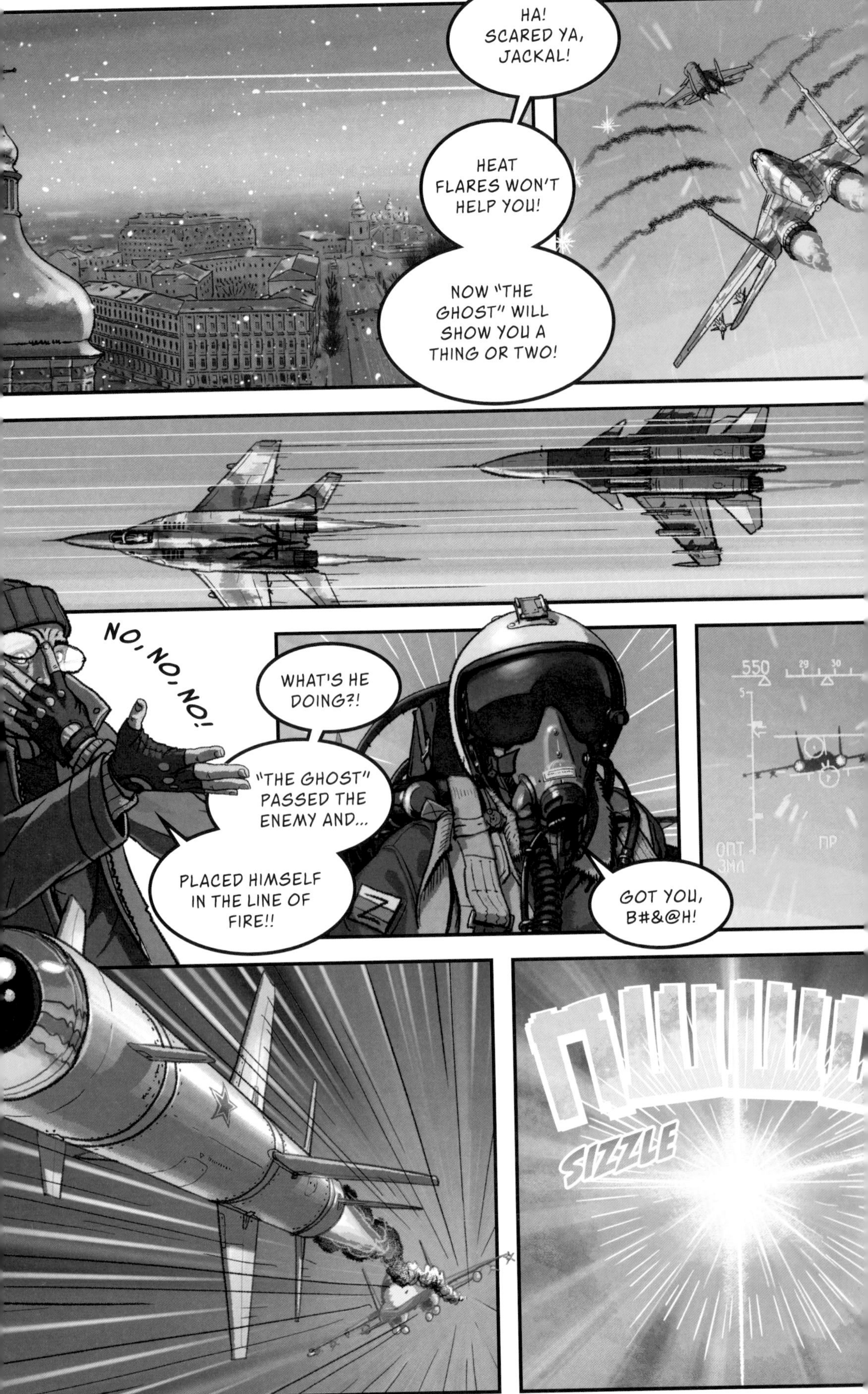
HA! SCARED YA, JACKAL!
HEAT FLARES WON'T HELP YOU!
NOW "THE GHOST" WILL SHOW YOU A THING OR TWO!
NO, NO, NO!
WHAT'S HE DOING?!
"THE GHOST" PASSED THE ENEMY AND...
PLACED HIMSELF IN THE LINE OF FIRE!!
GOT YOU, B#&@H!
SIZZLE

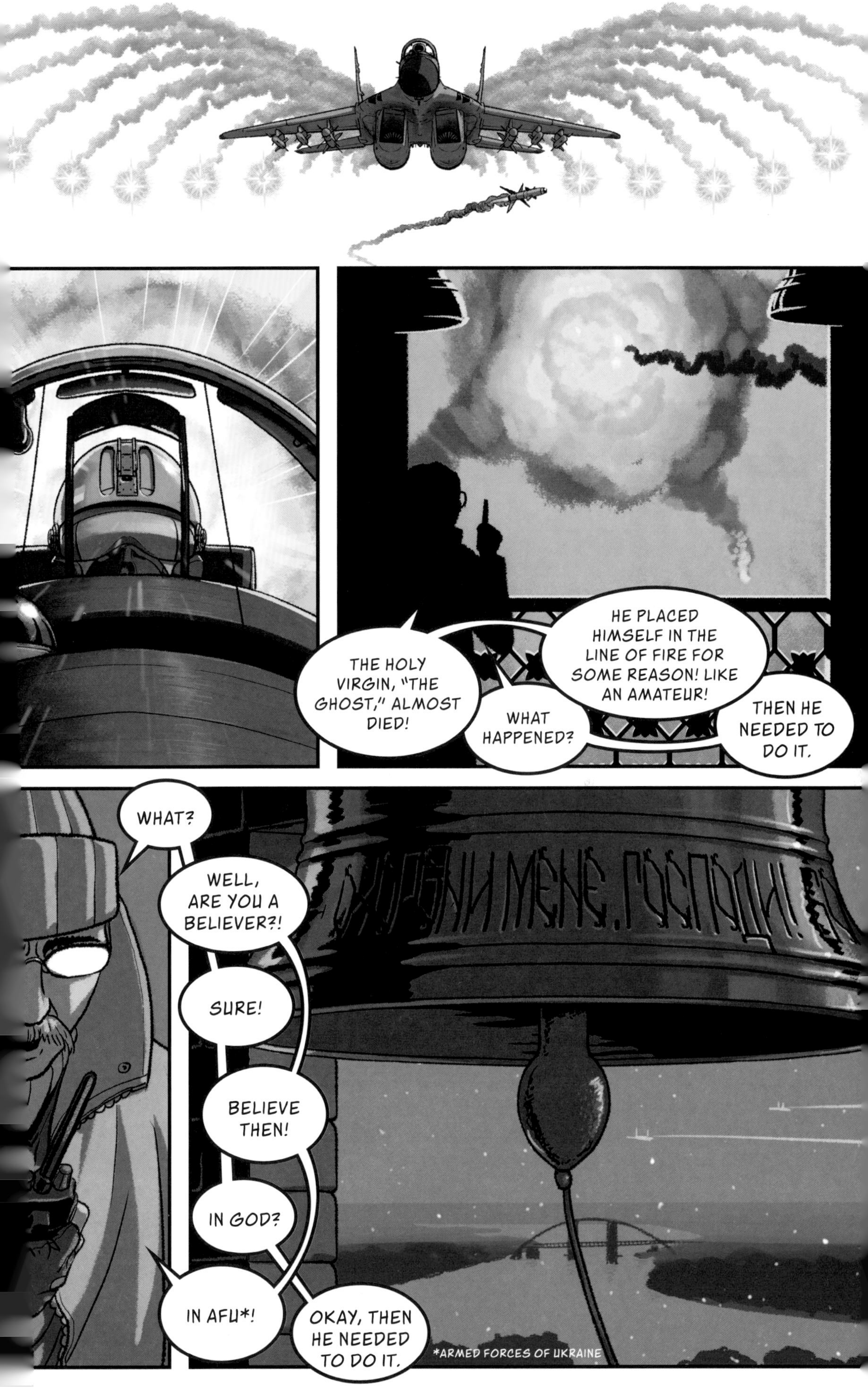
THE HOLY VIRGIN, "THE GHOST," ALMOST DIED!
WHAT HAPPENED?
HE PLACED HIMSELF IN THE LINE OF FIRE FOR SOME REASON! LIKE AN AMATEUR!
THEN HE NEEDED TO DO IT.
WHAT?
WELL, ARE YOU A BELIEVER?!
SURE!
BELIEVE THEN!
IN GOD?
IN AFU*!
OKAY, THEN HE NEEDED TO DO IT.
*ARMED FORCES OF UKRAINE

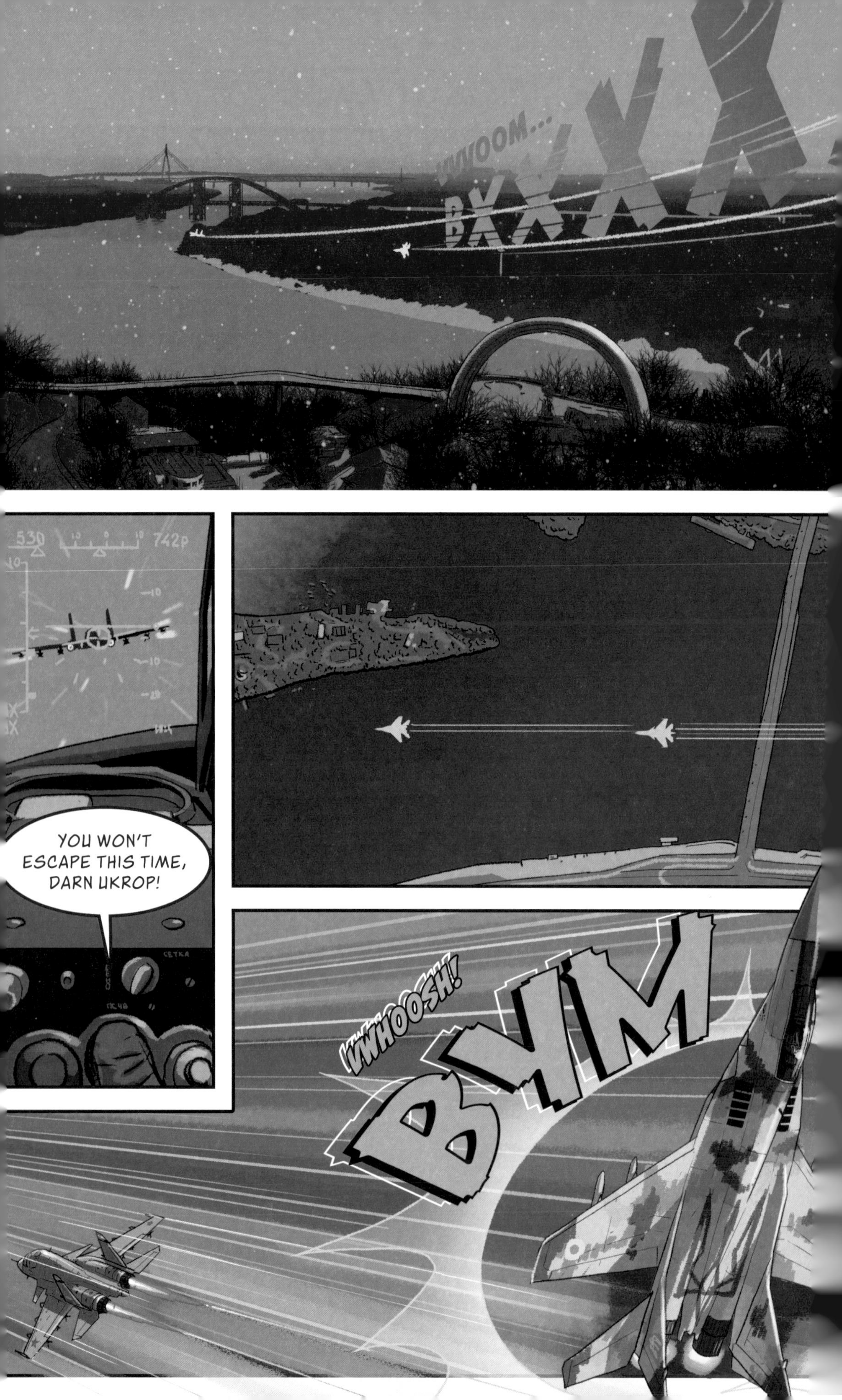

VWVOOM...
BXXX
YOU WON'T ESCAPE THIS TIME, DARN UKROP!
VWHOOSH!
BYIM

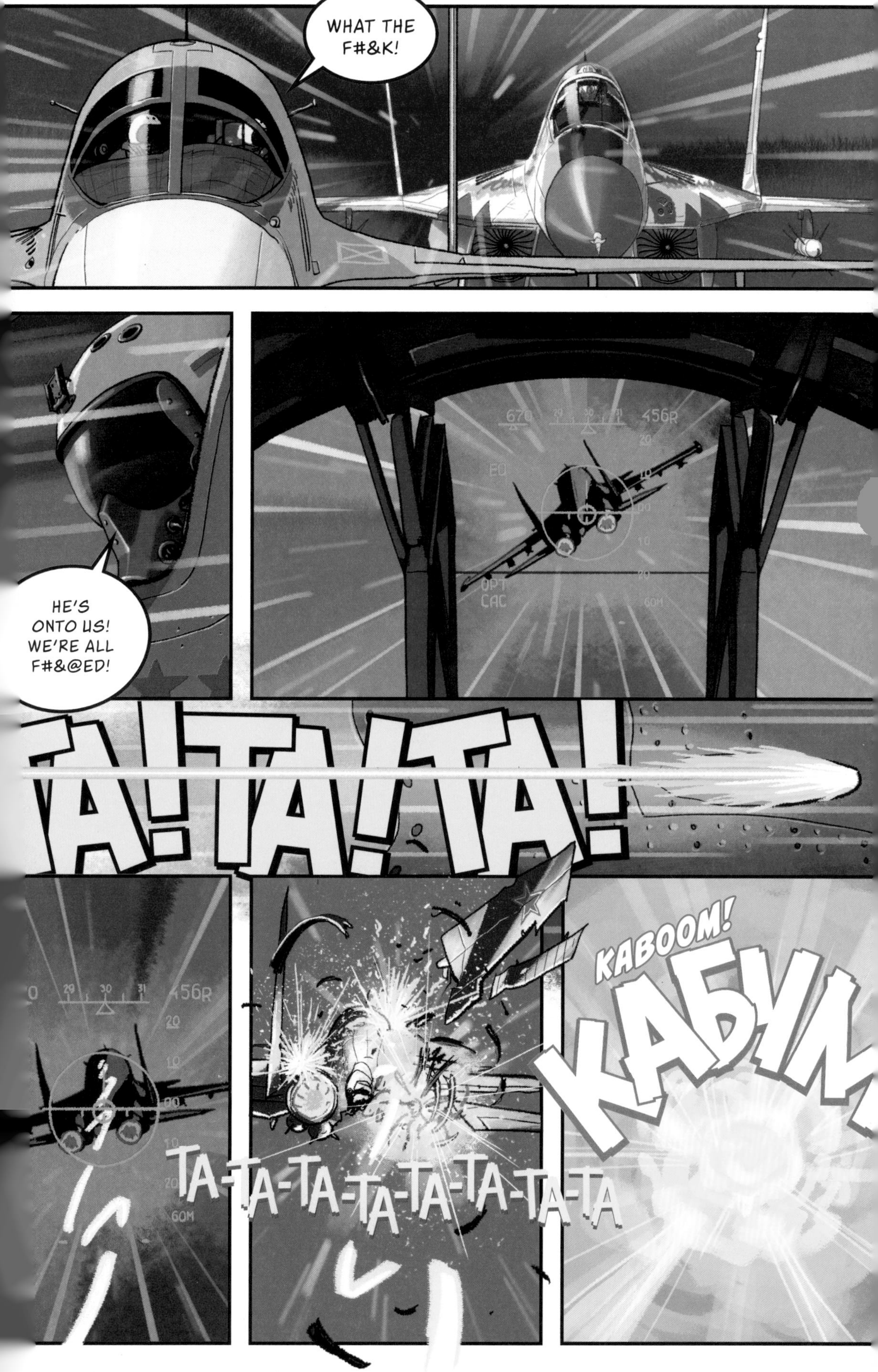
WHAT THE F#&K!
HE'S ONTO US! WE'RE ALL F#&@ED!
TA! TA! TA!
TA-TA-TA-TA-TA-TA-TA-TA
KABOOM!
КАБУМ

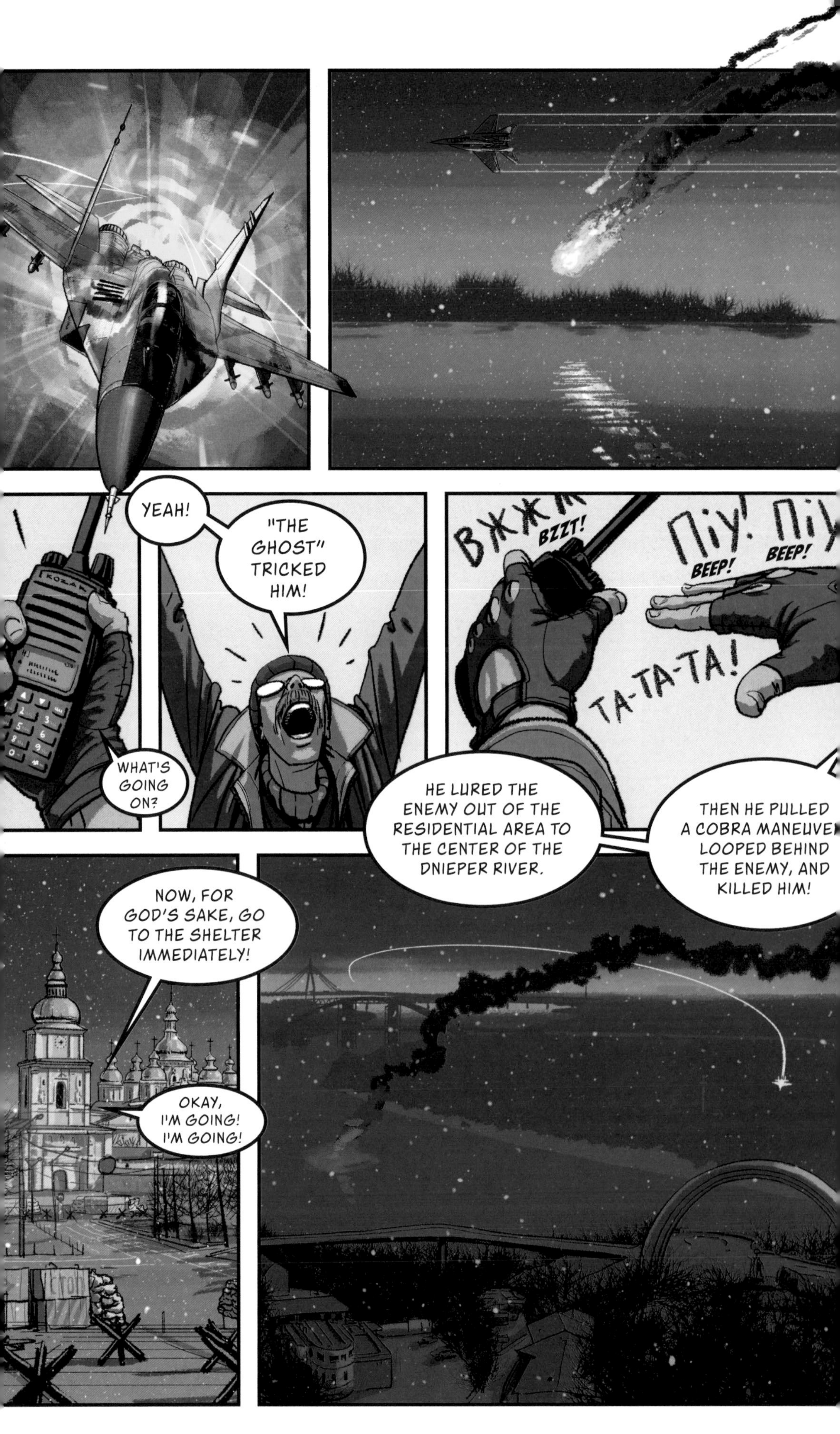

YEAH!
WHAT'S GOING ON?
"THE GHOST" TRICKED HIM!
ВЖЖЖ
BZZT!
Піу! Піу
BEEP!
BEEP!
TA-TA-TA!
HE LURED THE ENEMY OUT OF THE RESIDENTIAL AREA TO THE CENTER OF THE DNIEPER RIVER.
THEN HE PULLED A COBRA MANEUVE LOOPED BEHIND THE ENEMY, AND KILLED HIM!
NOW, FOR GOD'S SAKE, GO TO THE SHELTER IMMEDIATELY!
OKAY, I'M GOING! I'M GOING!

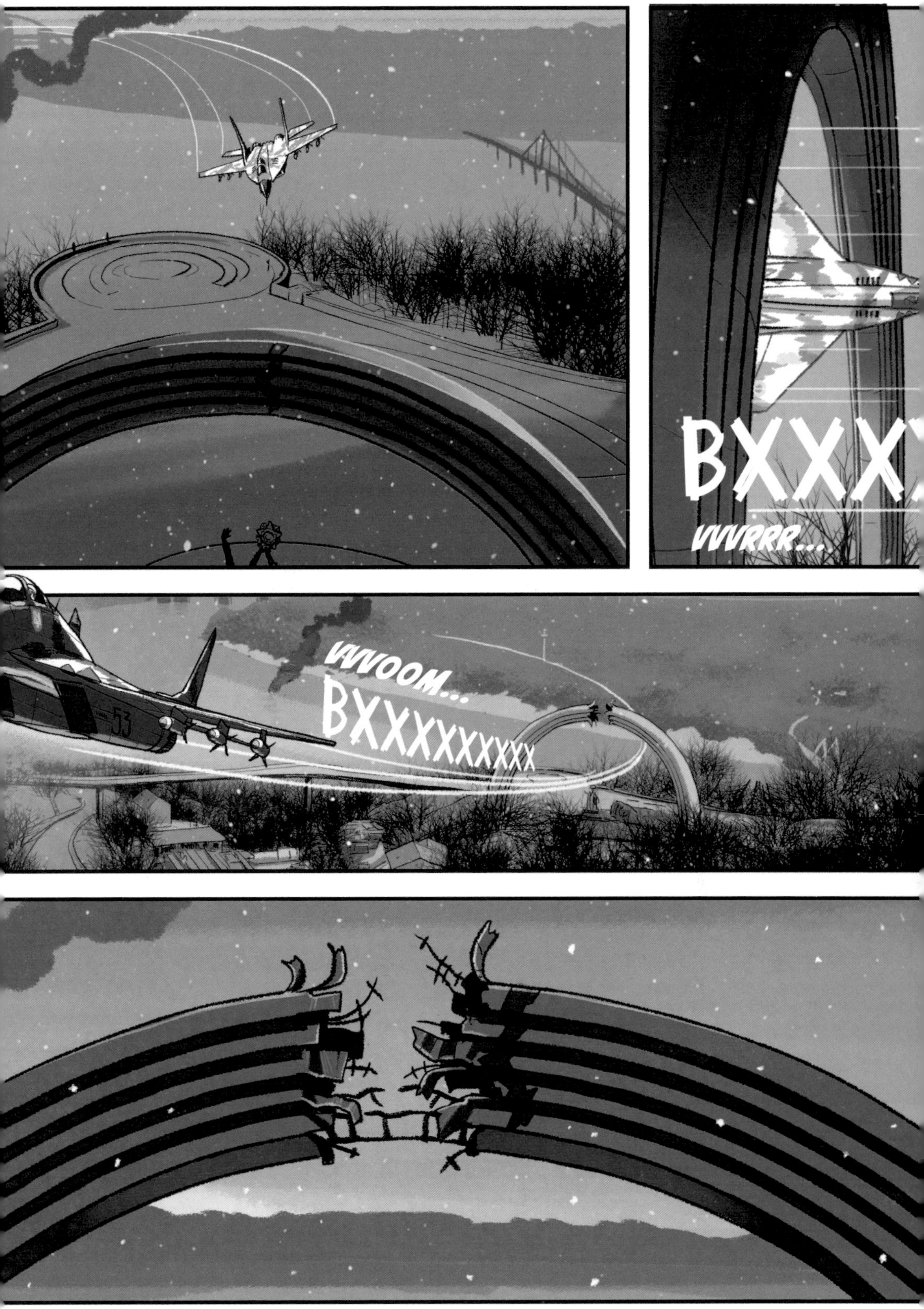
BXXXX
VVVRRR...
VVVOOM...
BXXXXXXXXXX

THE END.

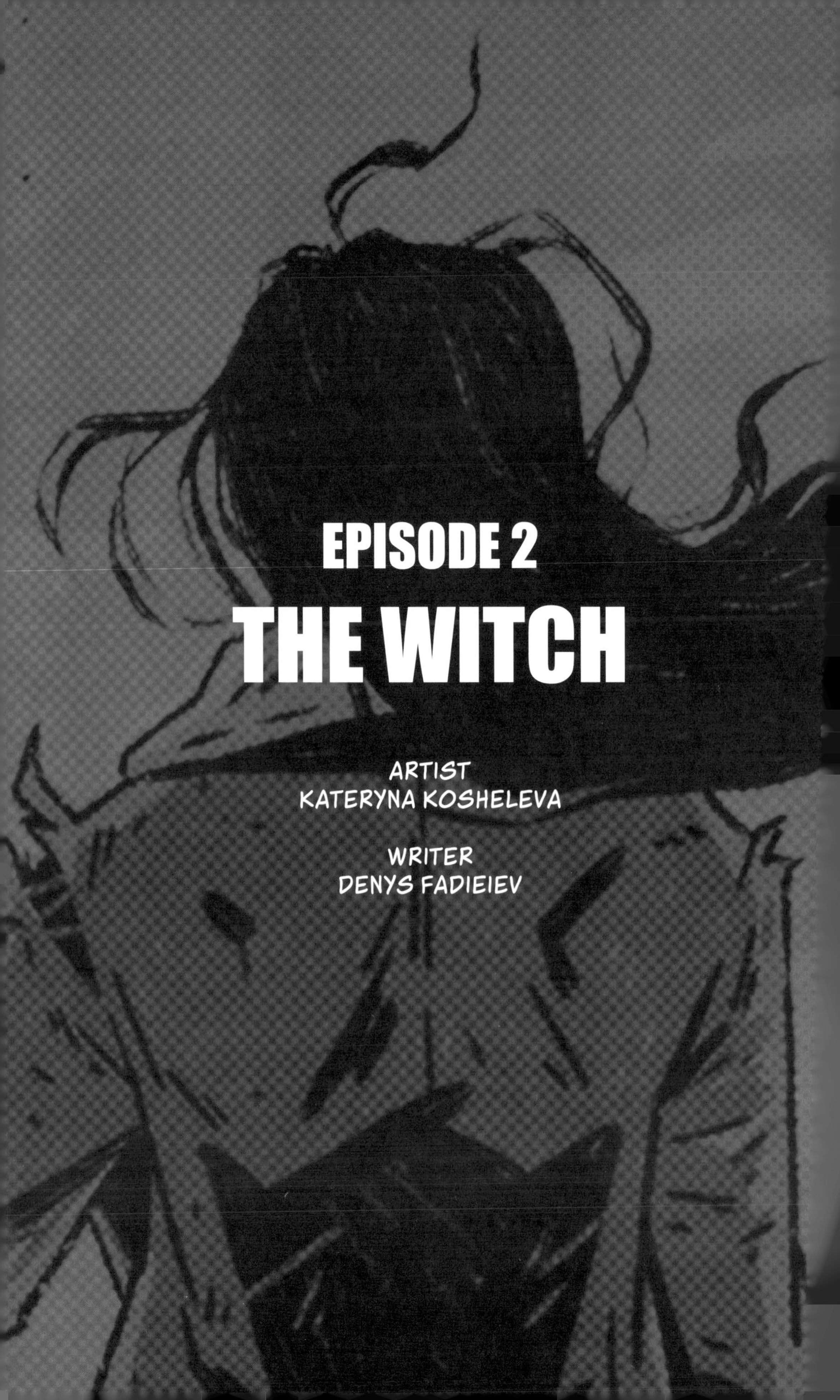
EPISODE 2
THE WITCH
ARTIST
KATERYNA KOSHELEVA
WRITER
DENYS FADIEIEV

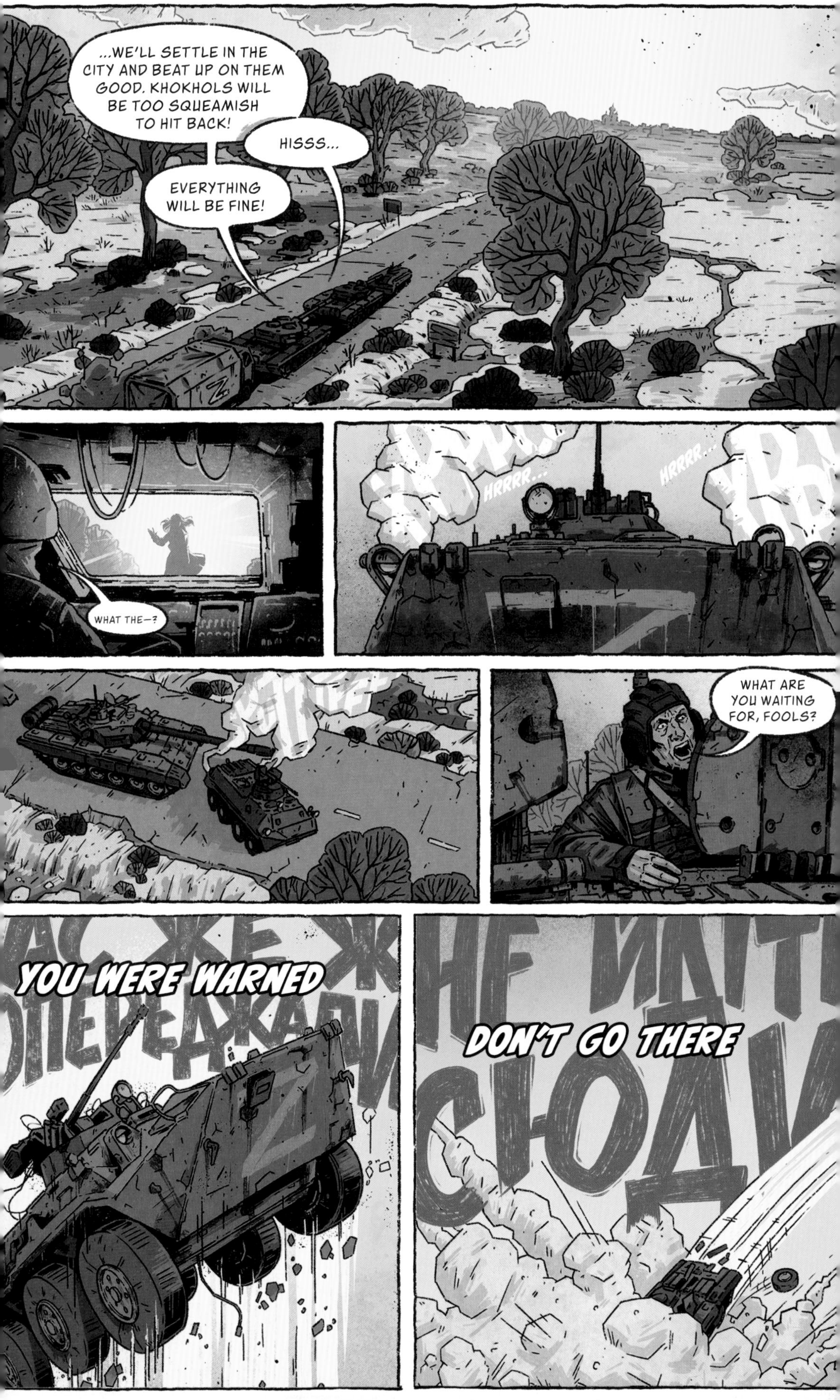
...WE'LL SETTLE IN THE CITY AND BEAT UP ON THEM GOOD. KHOKHOLS WILL BE TOO SQUEAMISH TO HIT BACK!
HISSS...
EVERYTHING WILL BE FINE!
WHAT THE—?
HRRRR...
HRRRR...
WHAT ARE YOU WAITING FOR, FOOLS?
YOU WERE WARNED
DON'T GO THERE

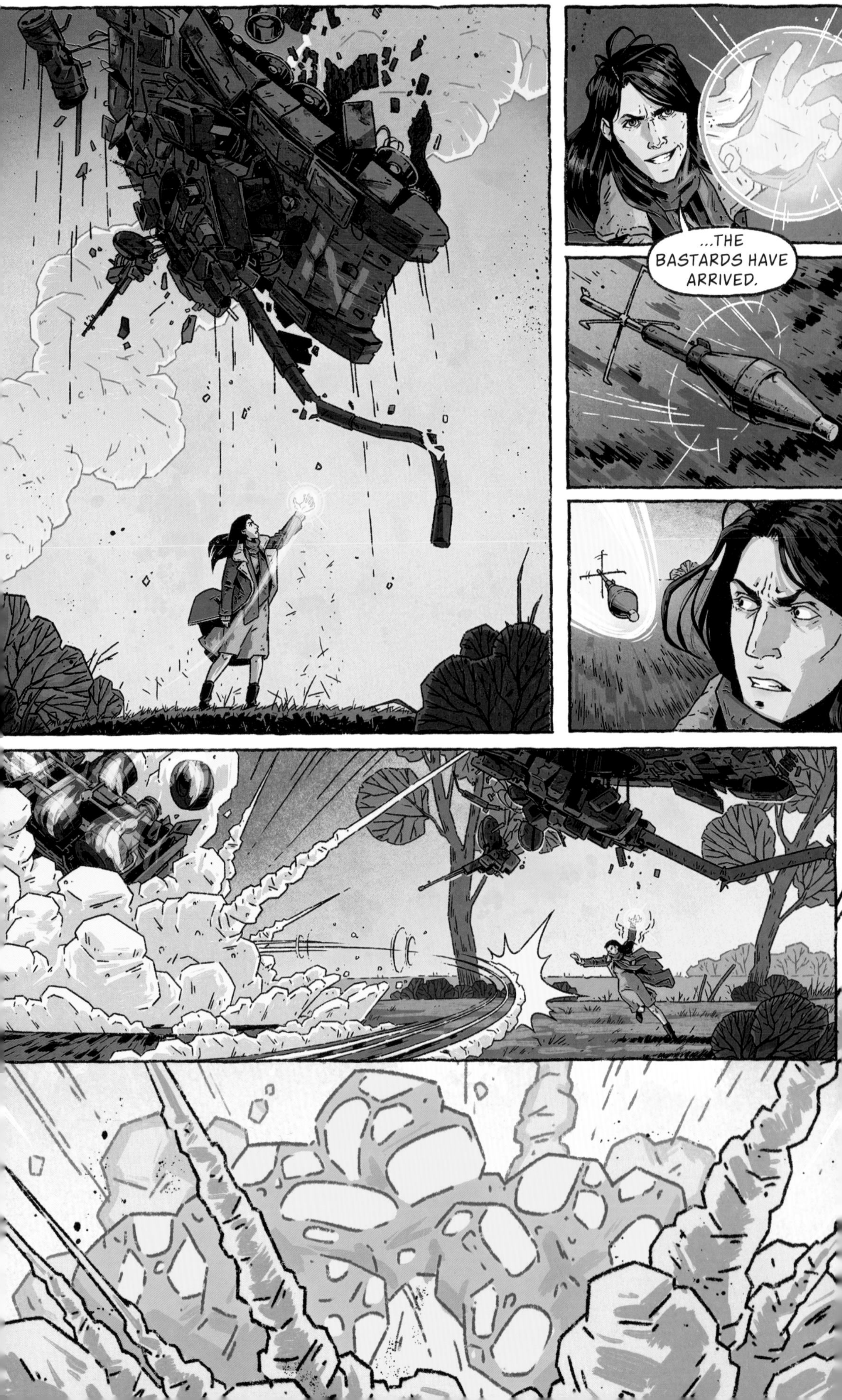
...THE BASTARDS HAVE ARRIVED.

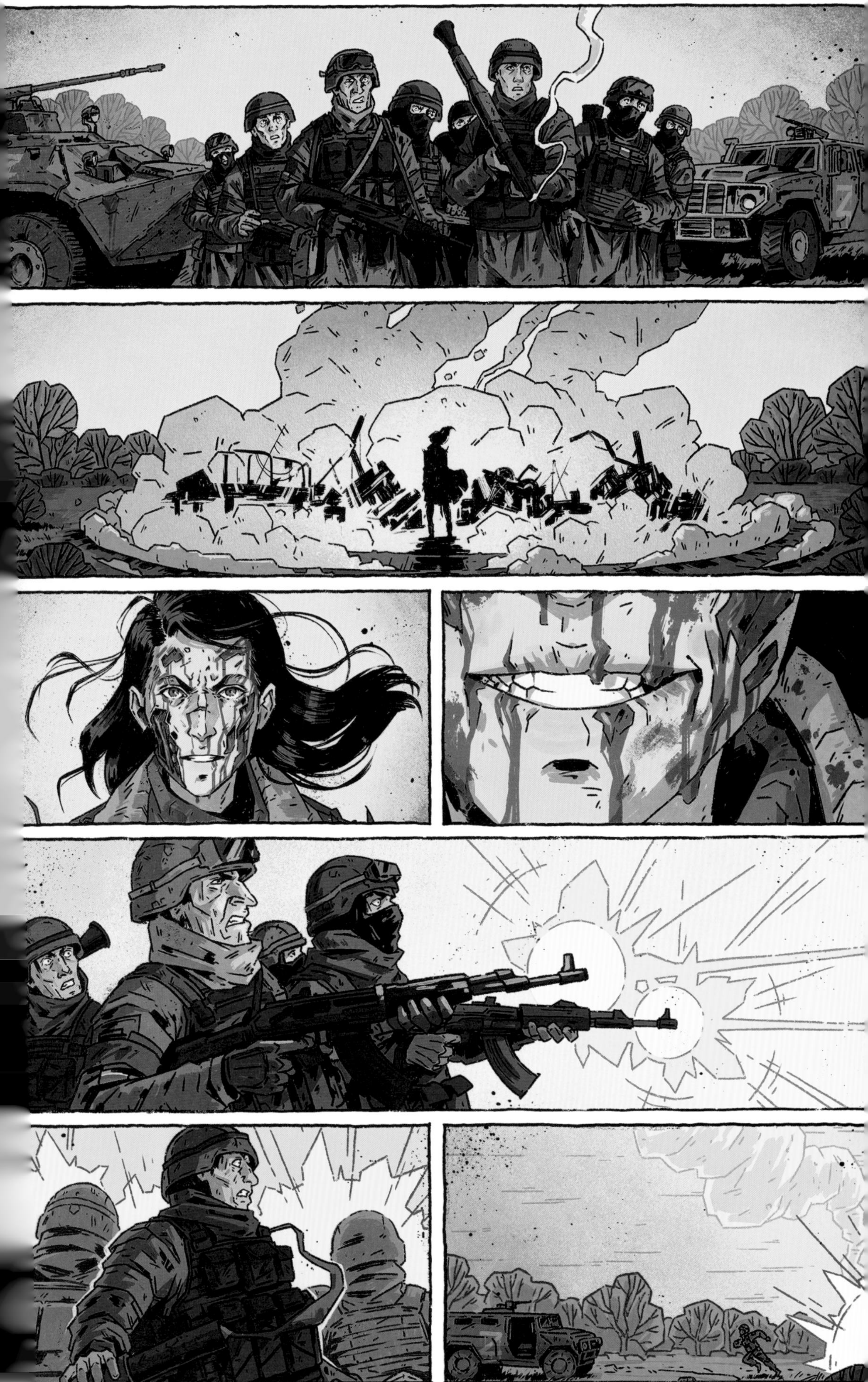

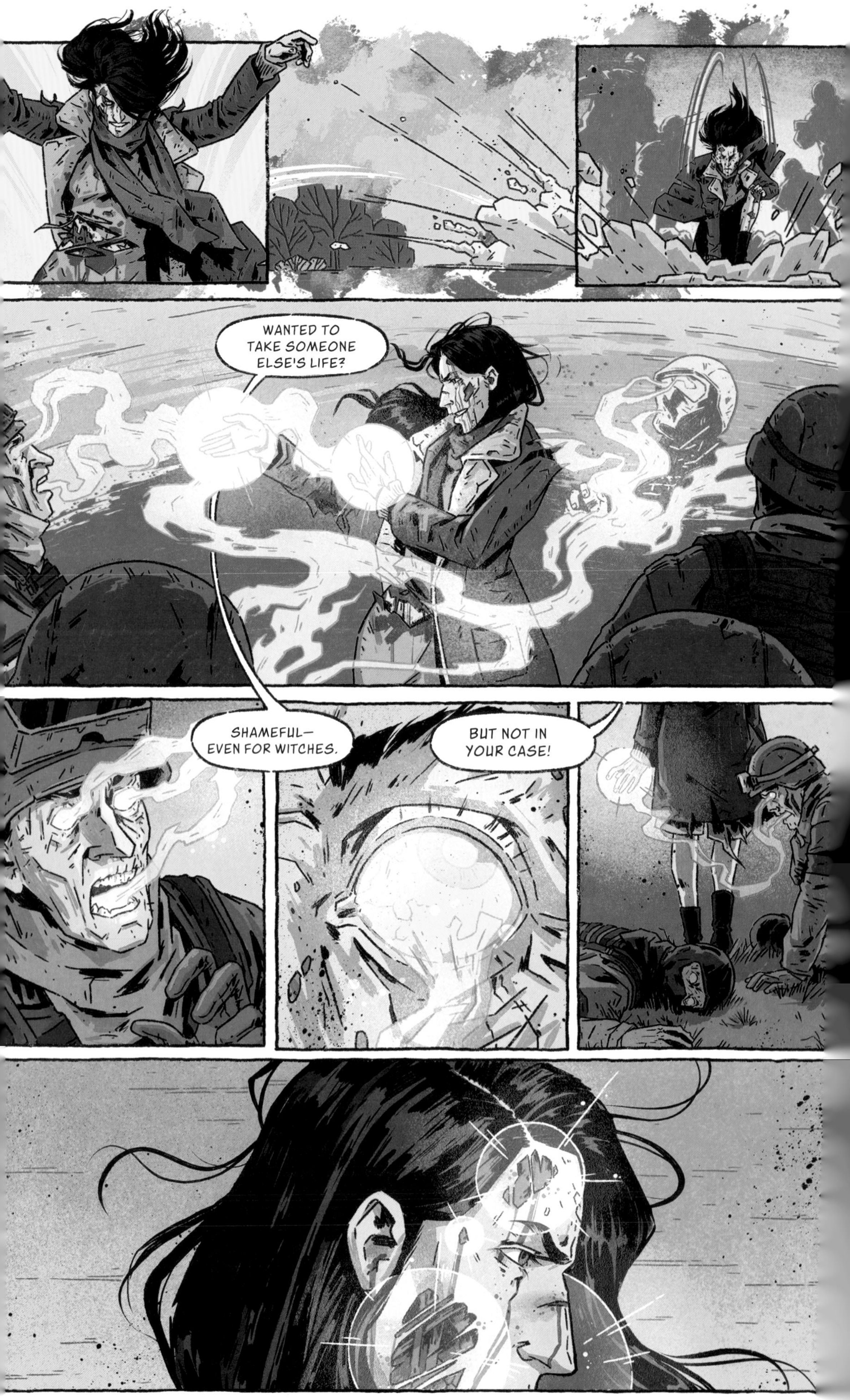
WANTED TO TAKE SOMEONE ELSE'S LIFE?
SHAMEFUL— EVEN FOR WITCHES.
BUT NOT IN YOUR CASE!

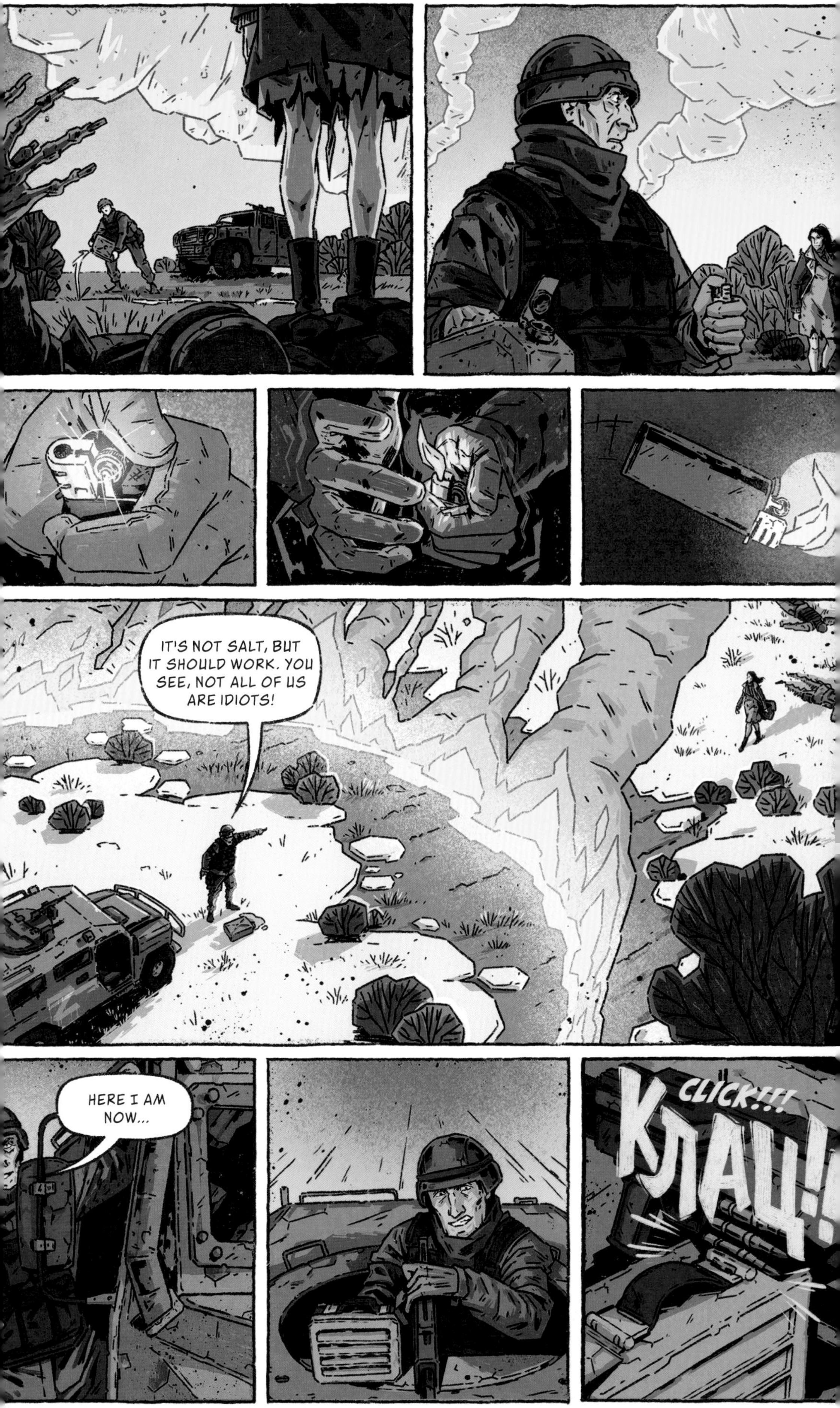
IT'S NOT SALT, BUT IT SHOULD WORK. YOU SEE, NOT ALL OF US ARE IDIOTS!
HERE I AM NOW...
CLICK!!!
КЛАЦ!!

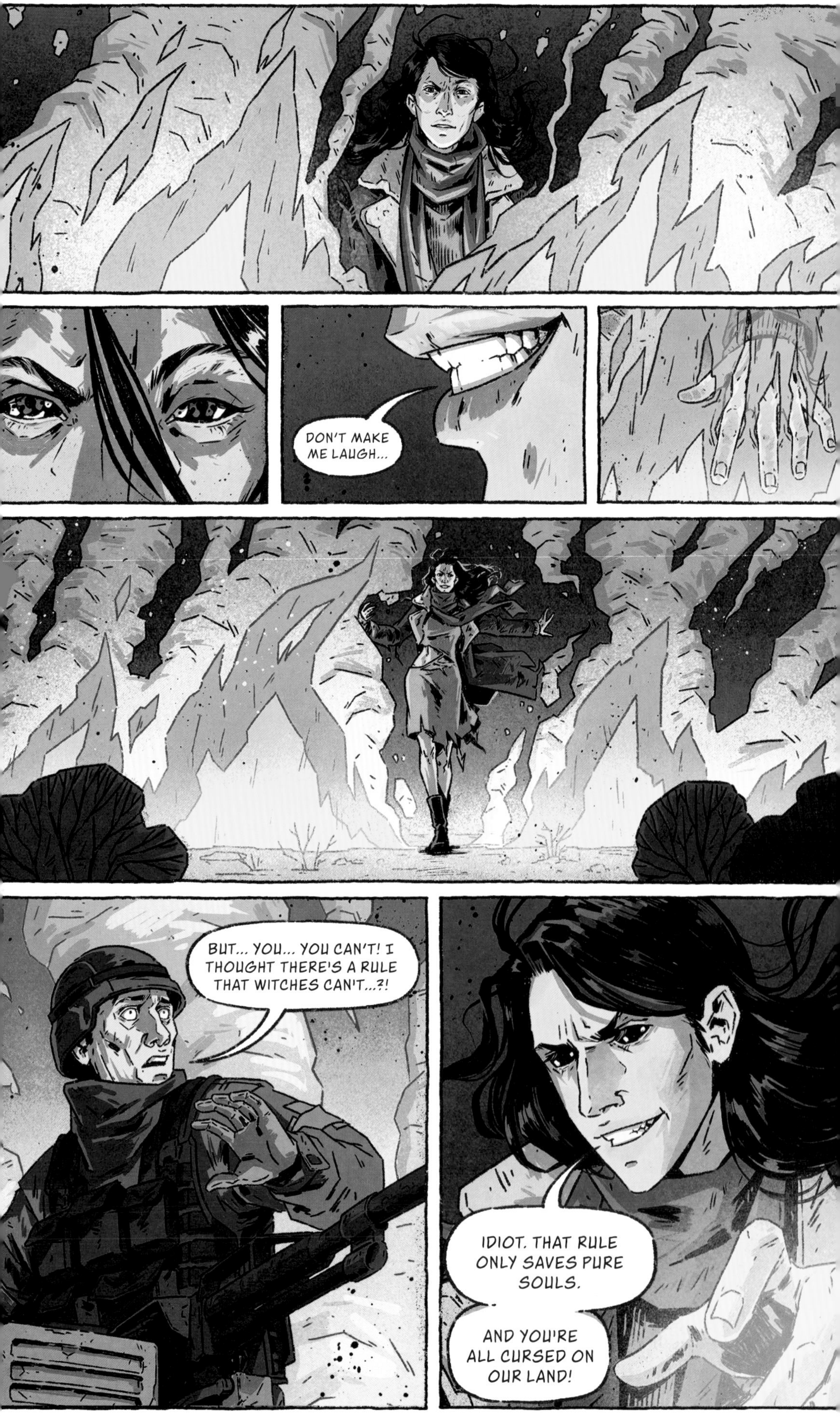
DON'T MAKE ME LAUGH...
BUT... YOU... YOU CAN'T! I THOUGHT THERE'S A RULE THAT WITCHES CAN'T...?!
IDIOT. THAT RULE ONLY SAVES PURE SOULS.
AND YOU'RE ALL CURSED ON OUR LAND!

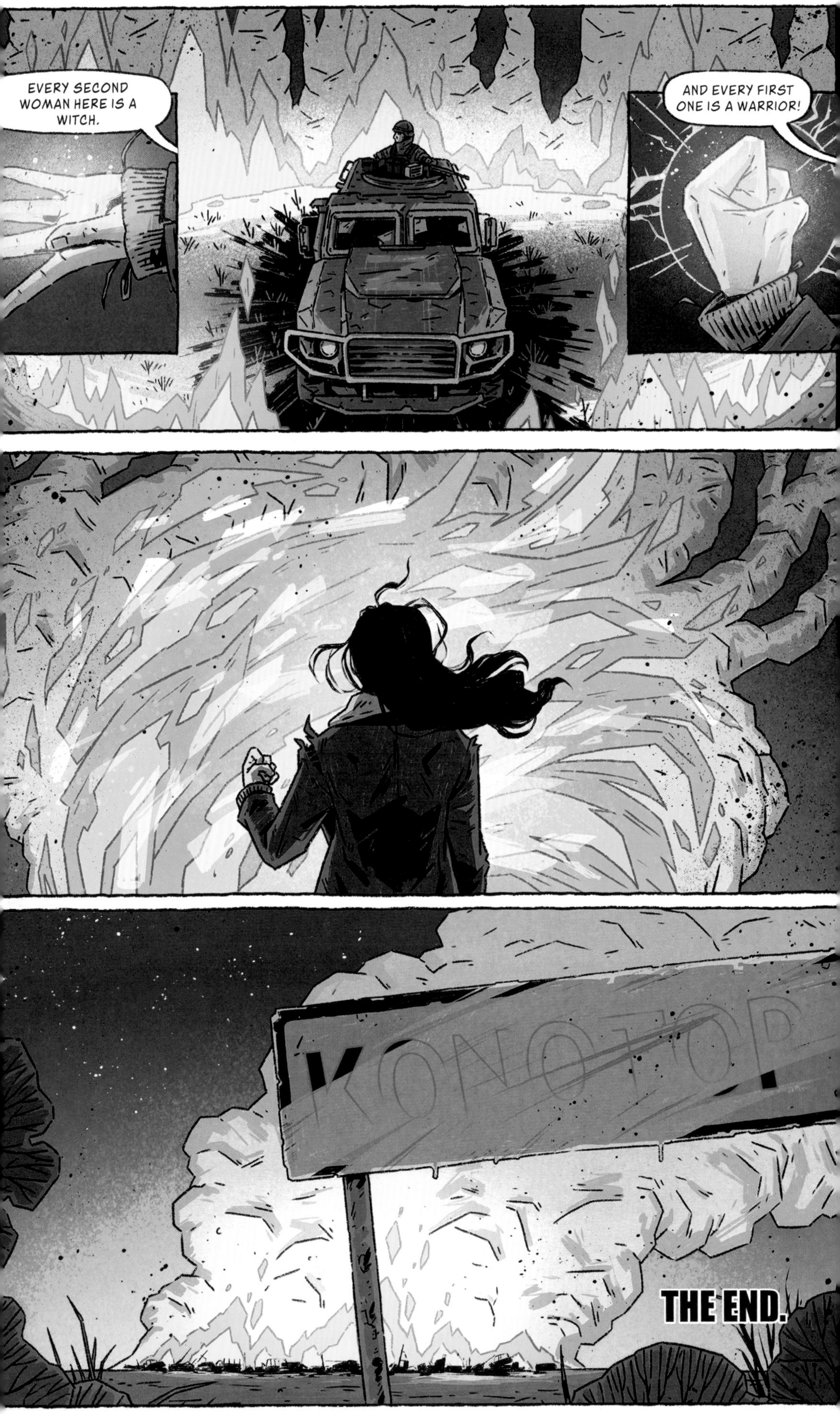
EVERY SECOND WOMAN HERE IS A WITCH.
AND EVERY FIRST ONE IS A WARRIOR!
KONOTOP
THE END.

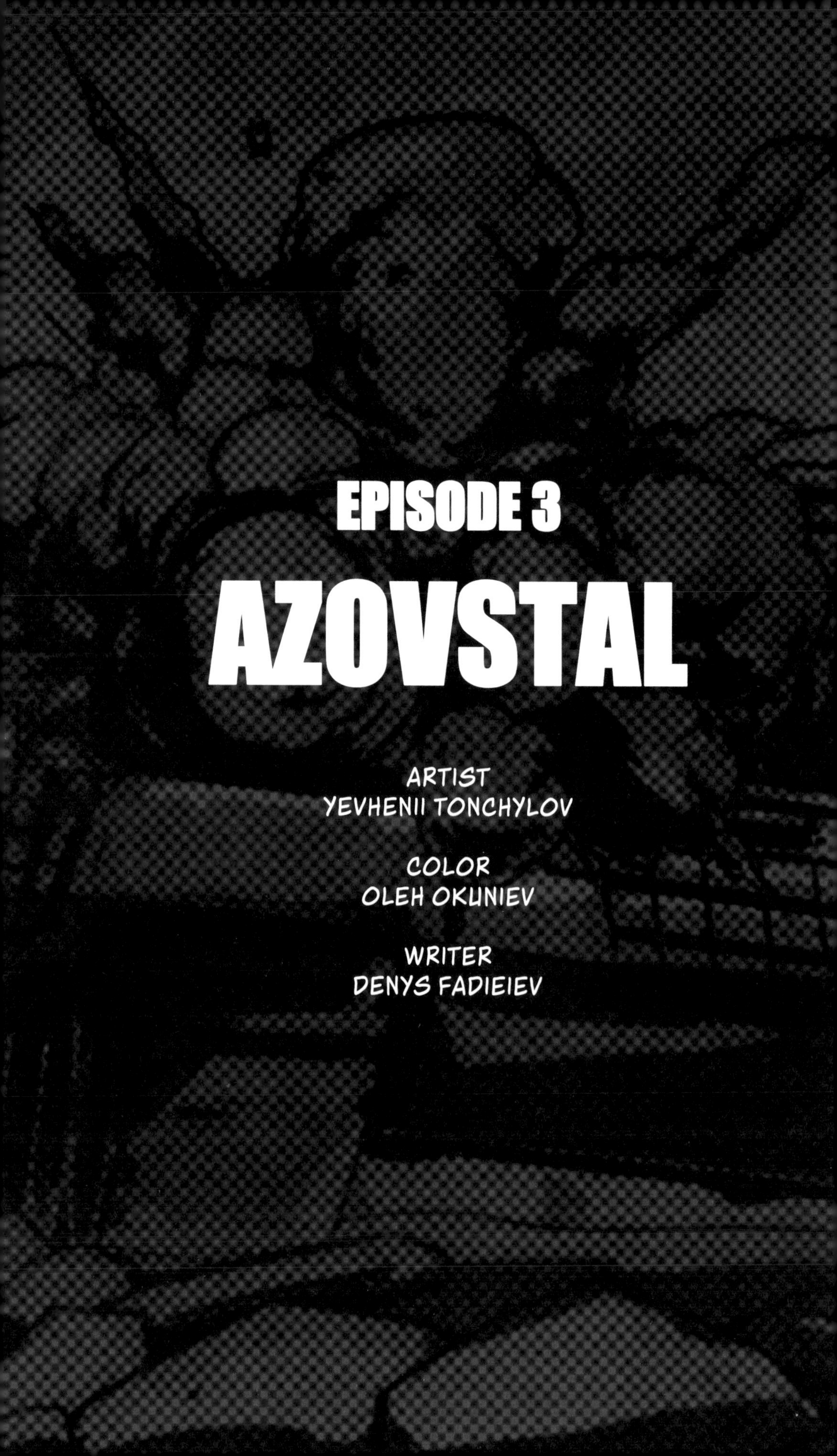

EPISODE 3

AZOVSTAL

ARTIST
YEVHENII TONCHYLOV

COLOR
OLEH OKUNIEV

WRITER
DENYS FADIEIEV

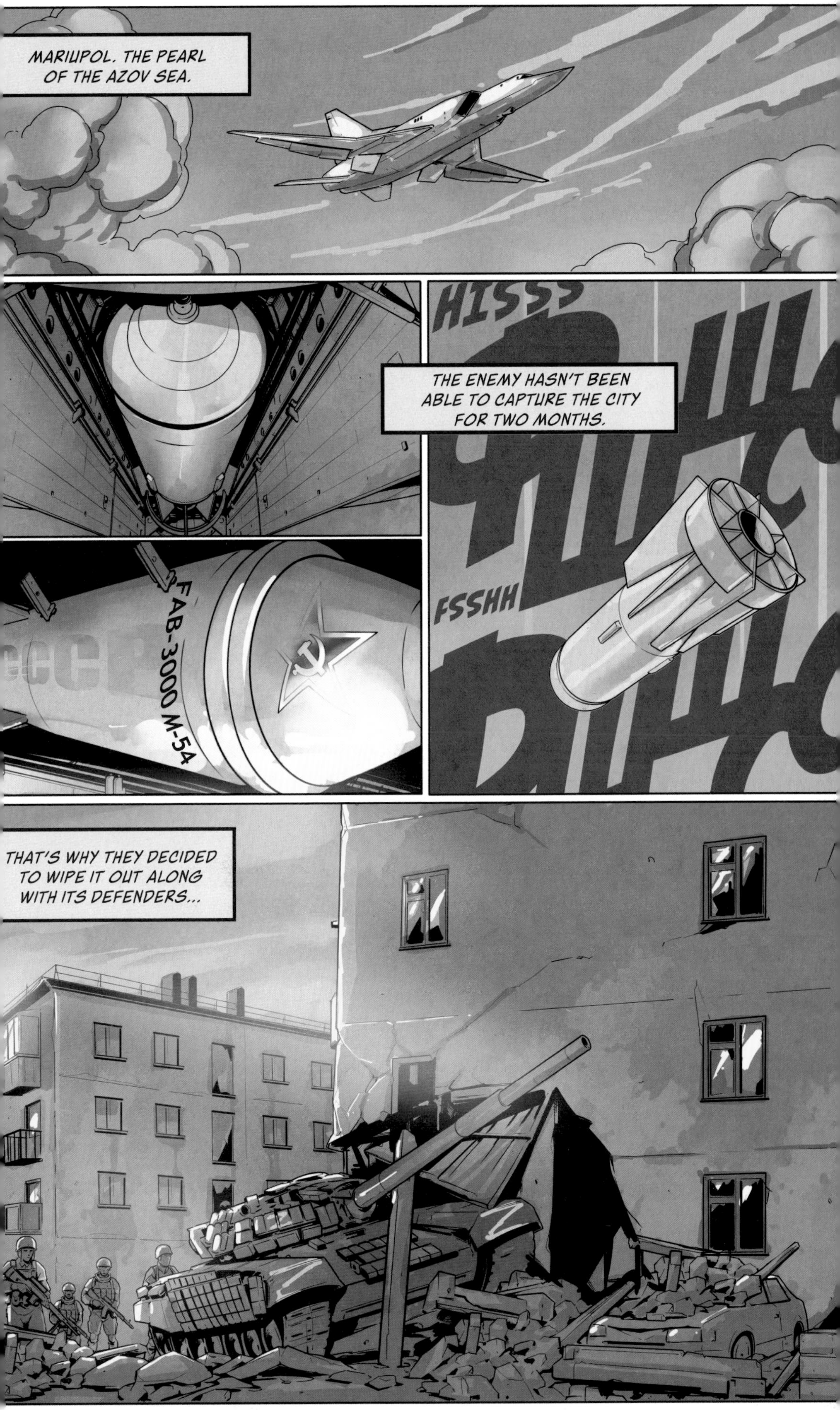
MARIUPOL. THE PEARL OF THE AZOV SEA.
HISSS
THE ENEMY HASN'T BEEN ABLE TO CAPTURE THE CITY FOR TWO MONTHS.
FAB-3000 M-54
FSSHH
THAT'S WHY THEY DECIDED TO WIPE IT OUT ALONG WITH ITS DEFENDERS...

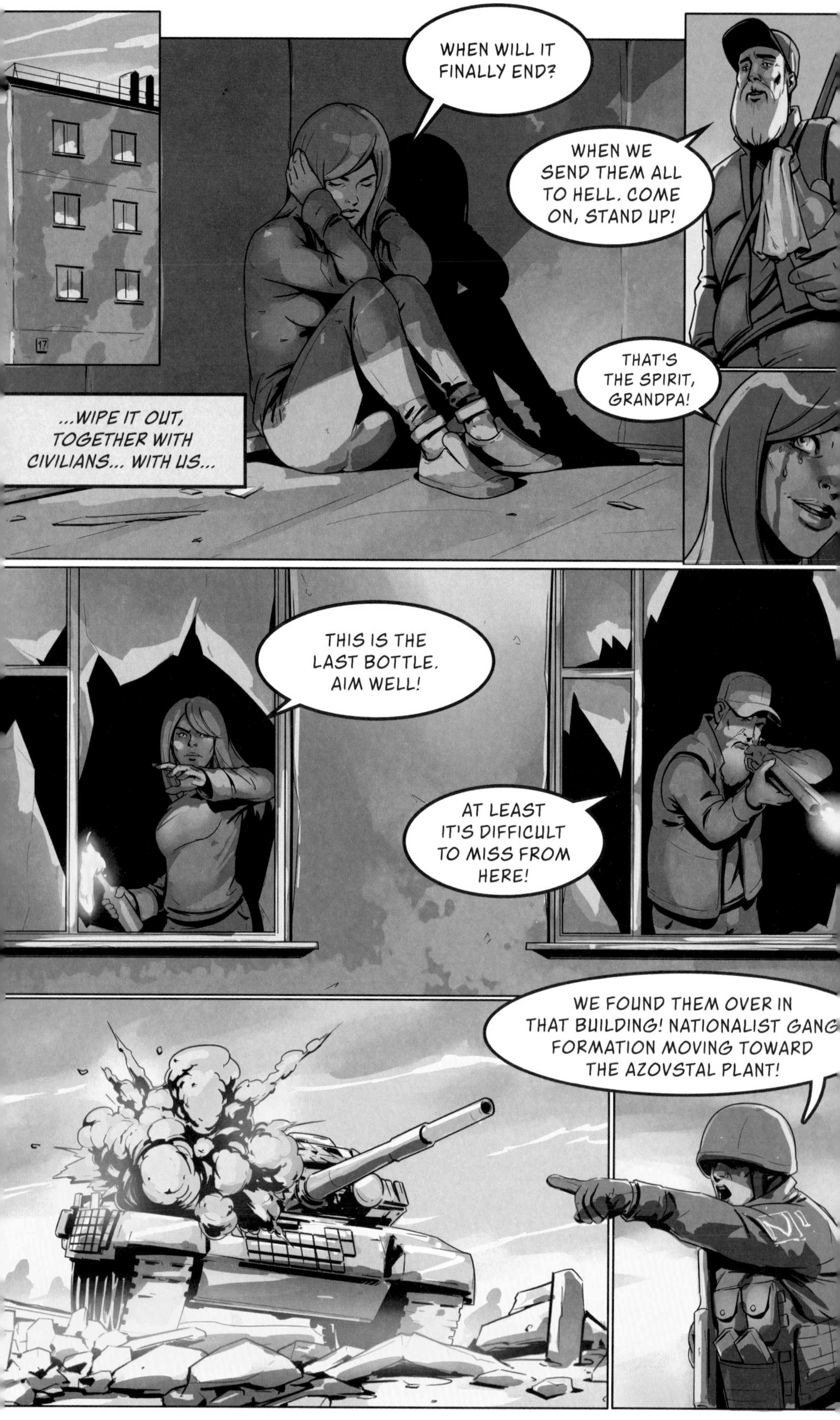

WHEN WILL IT FINALLY END?
WHEN WE SEND THEM ALL TO HELL. COME ON, STAND UP!
...WIPE IT OUT, TOGETHER WITH CIVILIANS... WITH US...
THAT'S THE SPIRIT, GRANDPA!
THIS IS THE LAST BOTTLE. AIM WELL!
AT LEAST IT'S DIFFICULT TO MISS FROM HERE!
WE FOUND THEM OVER IN THAT BUILDING! NATIONALIST GANG FORMATION MOVING TOWARD THE AZOVSTAL PLANT!

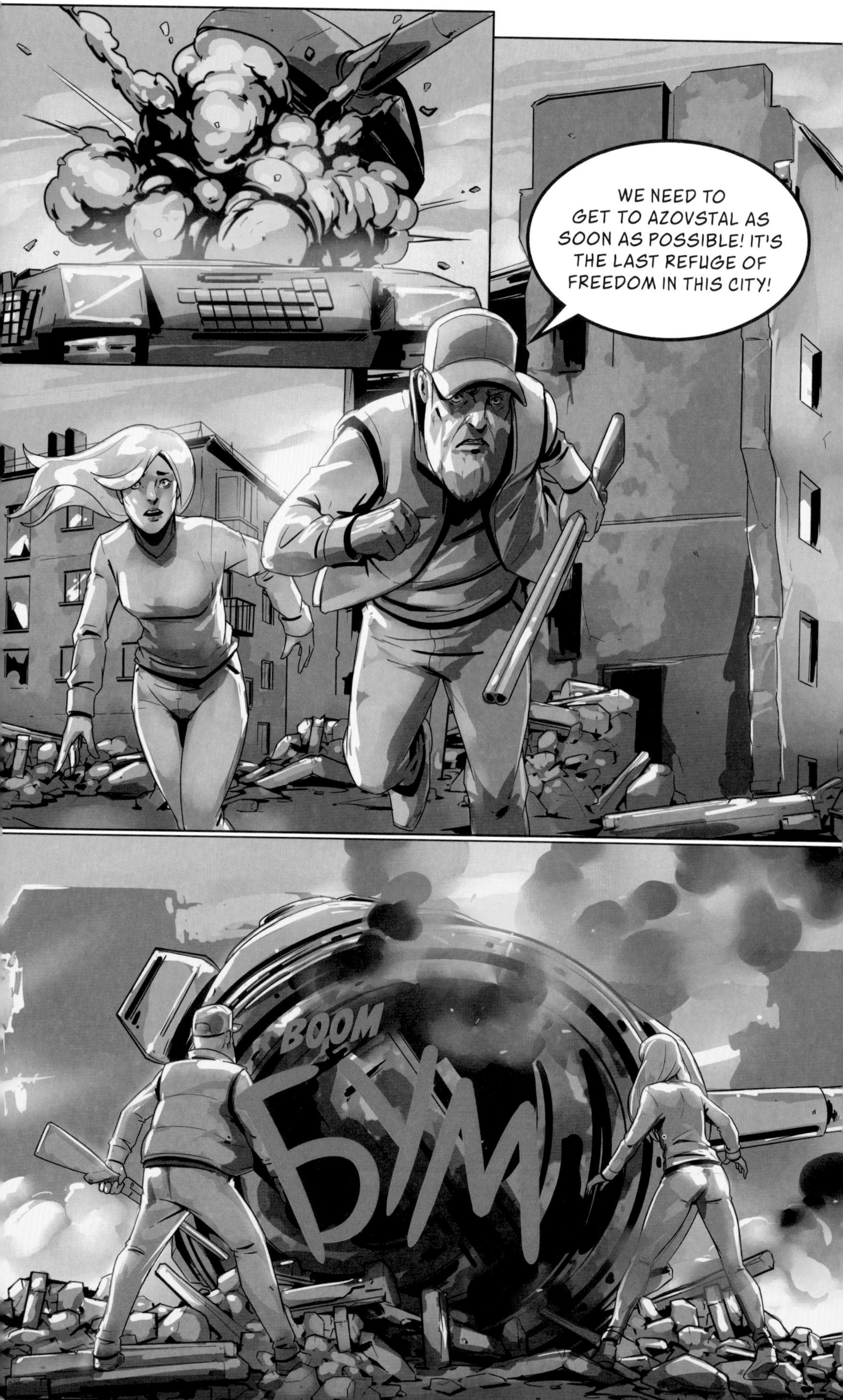
WE NEED TO GET TO AZOVSTAL AS SOON AS POSSIBLE! IT'S THE LAST REFUGE OF FREEDOM IN THIS CITY!
BOOM
БУМ

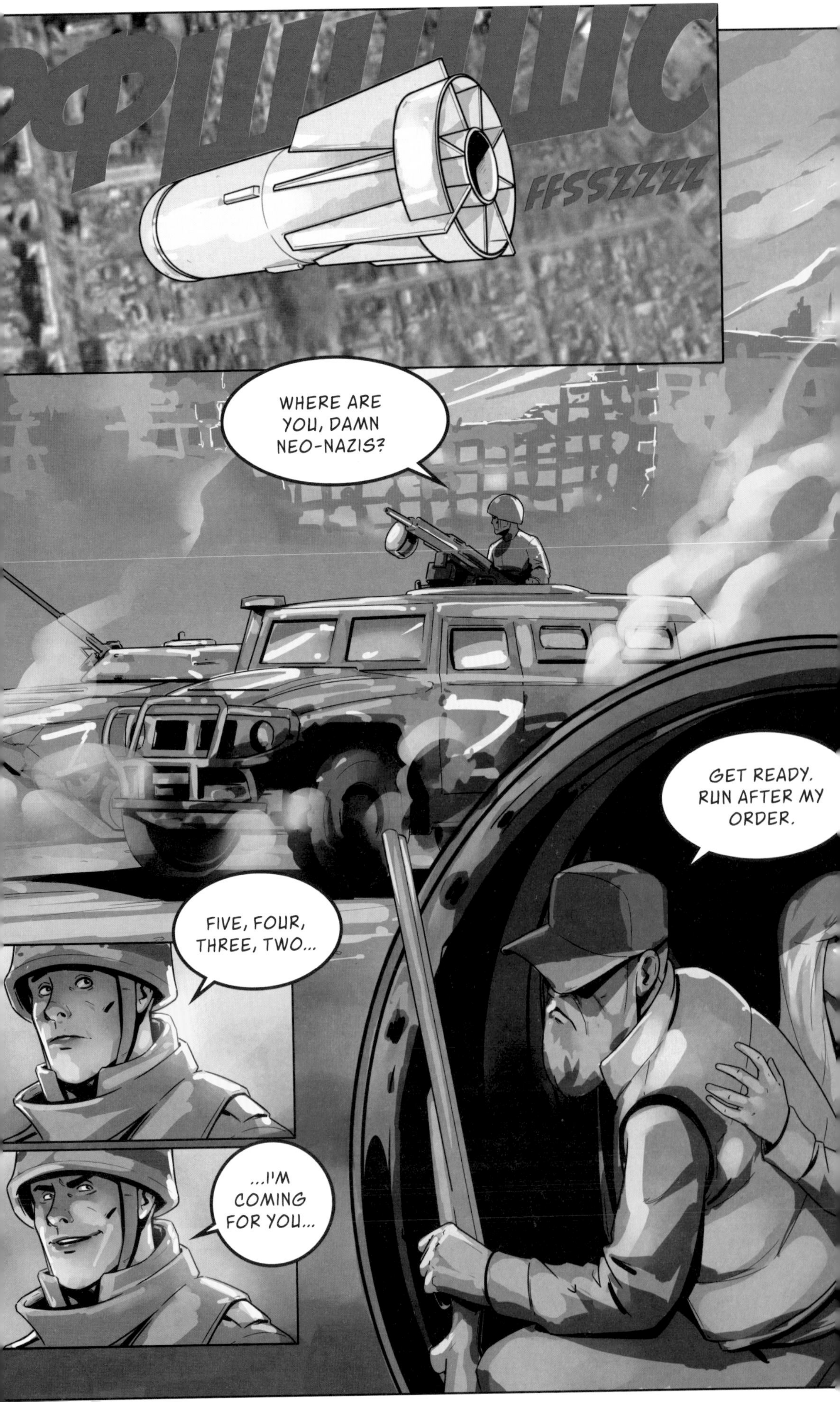

ФШШШШШС
FFSSZZZZ
WHERE ARE YOU, DAMN NEO-NAZIS?
GET READY. RUN AFTER MY ORDER.
FIVE, FOUR, THREE, TWO...
...I'M COMING FOR YOU...

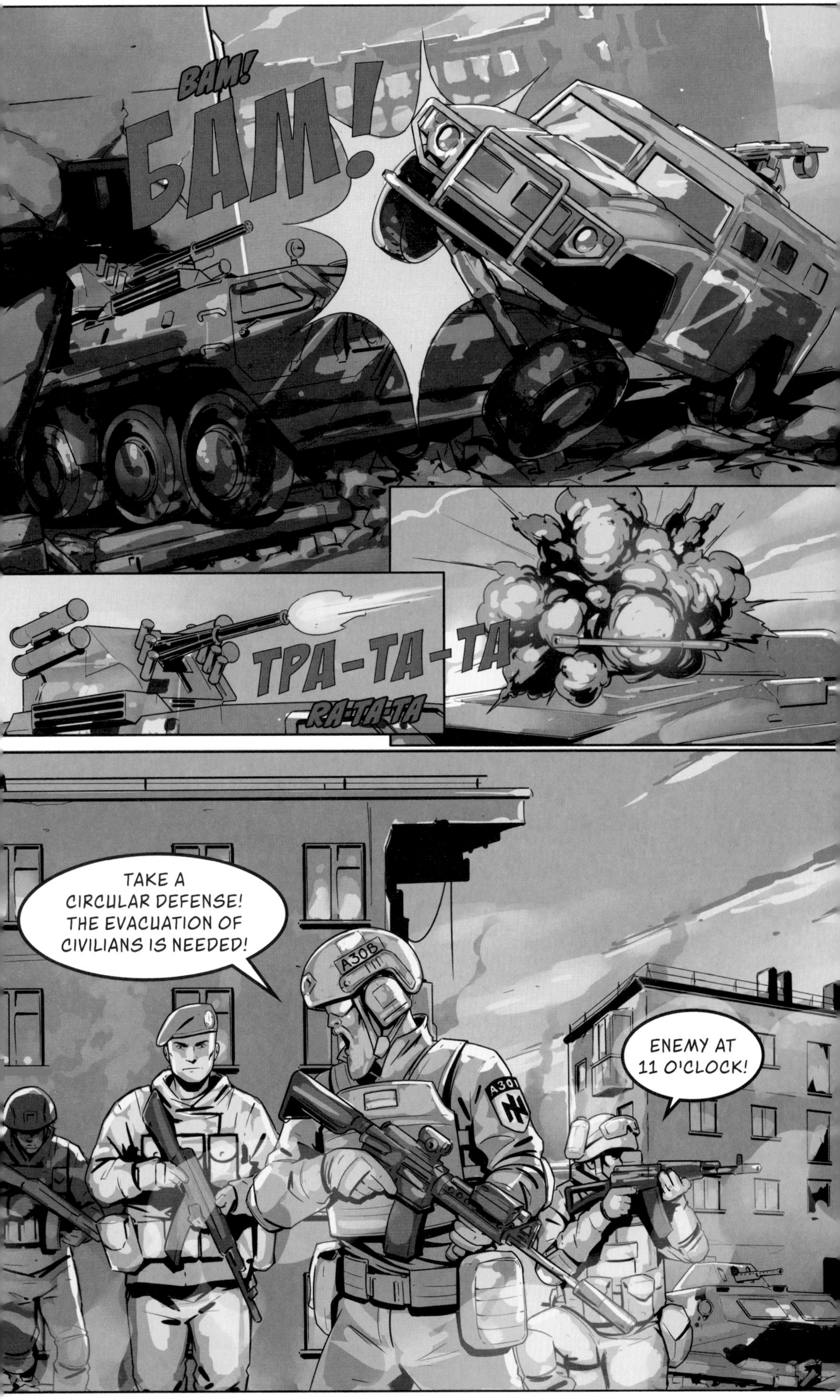
BAM!
БАМ!
ТРА-ТА-ТА
RA-TA-TA
TAKE A CIRCULAR DEFENSE! THE EVACUATION OF CIVILIANS IS NEEDED!
ENEMY AT 11 O'CLOCK!

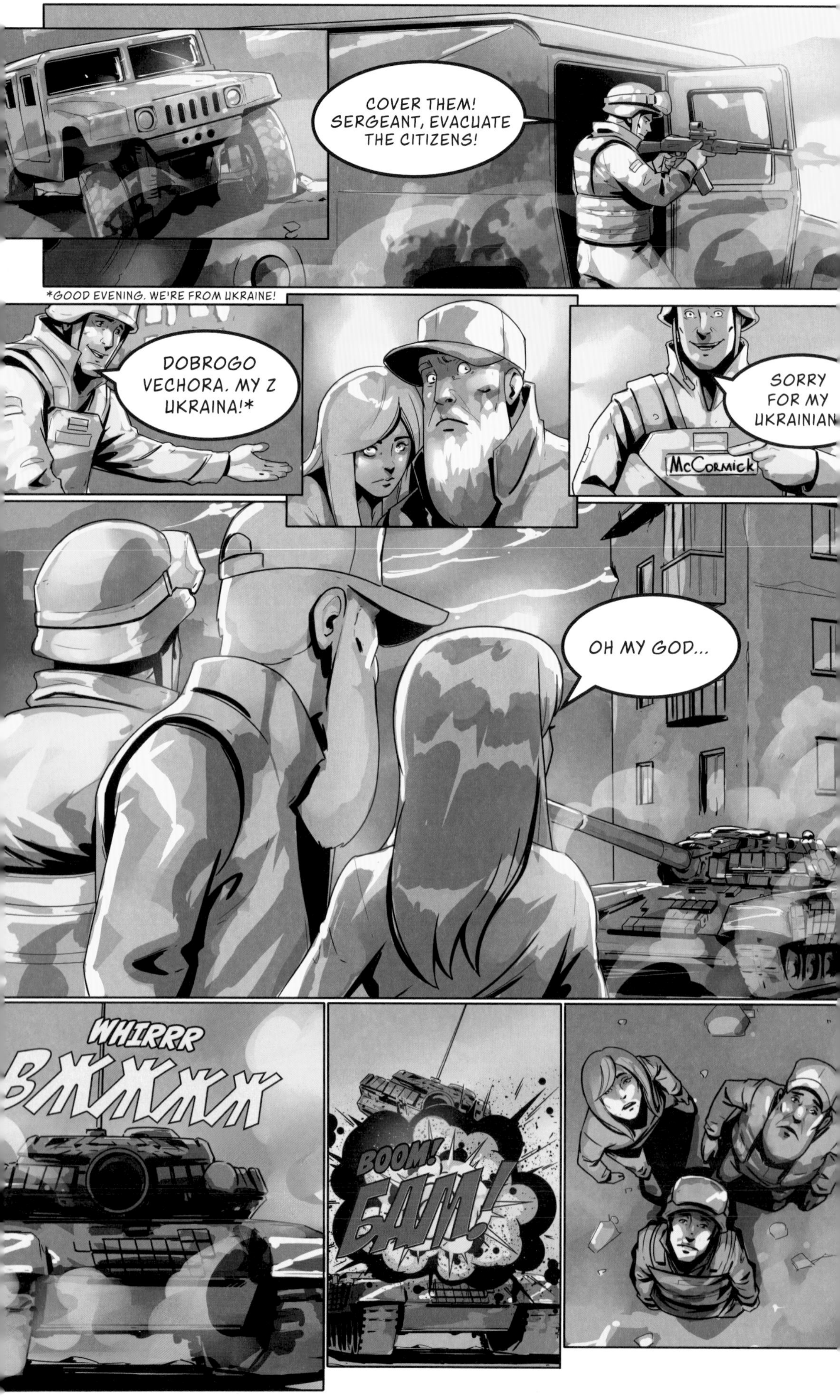
COVER THEM! SERGEANT, EVACUATE THE CITIZENS!
*GOOD EVENING. WE'RE FROM UKRAINE!
DOBROGO VECHORA. MY Z UKRAINA!*
SORRY FOR MY UKRAINIAN
McCormick
OH MY GOD...
WHIRRR
ВЖЖЖЖ
BOOM!
БАМ!

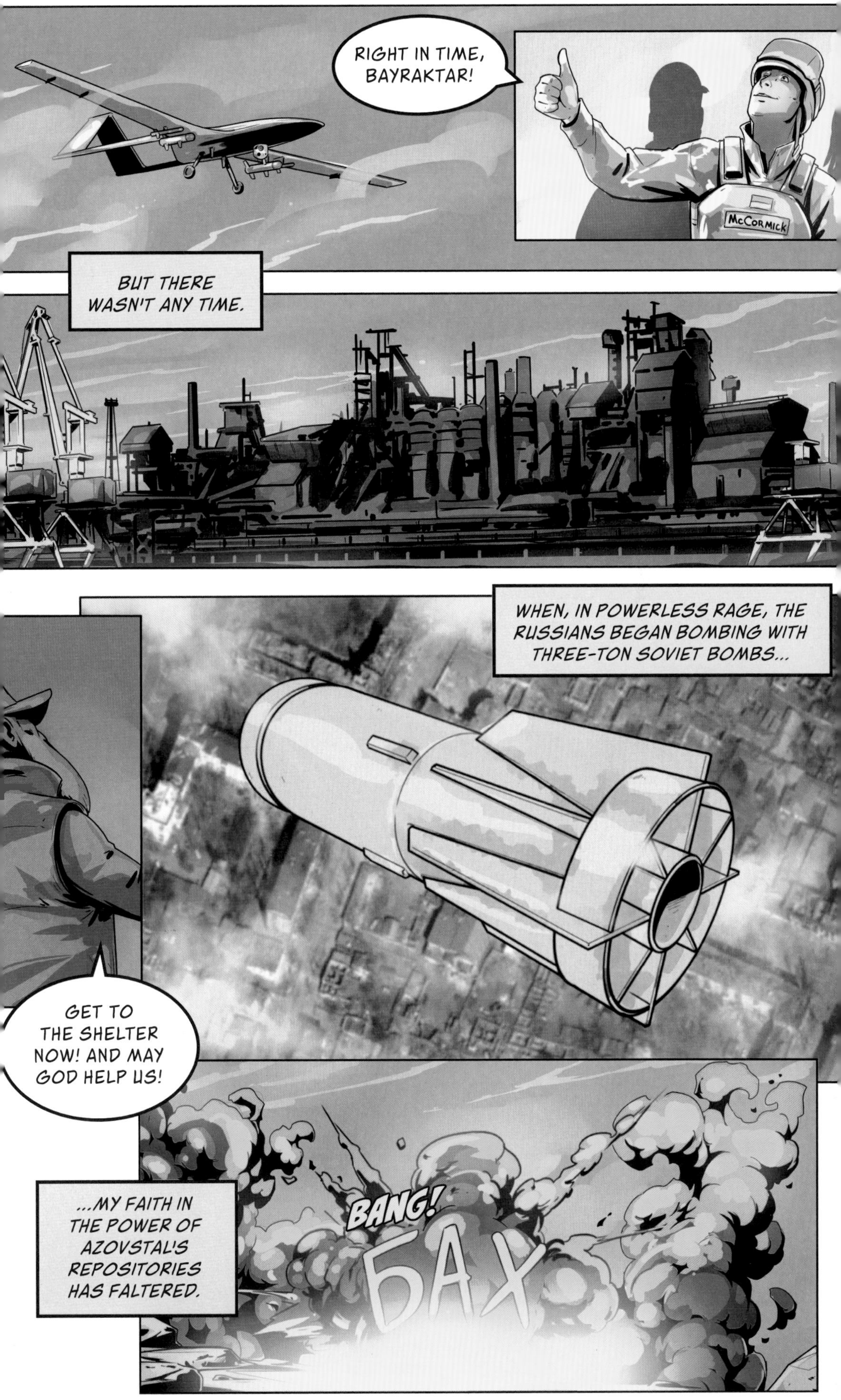
RIGHT IN TIME, BAYRAKTAR!
McCORMICK
BUT THERE WASN'T ANY TIME.
WHEN, IN POWERLESS RAGE, THE RUSSIANS BEGAN BOMBING WITH THREE-TON SOVIET BOMBS...
GET TO THE SHELTER NOW! AND MAY GOD HELP US!
...MY FAITH IN THE POWER OF AZOVSTAL'S REPOSITORIES HAS FALTERED.
BANG!
БАХ

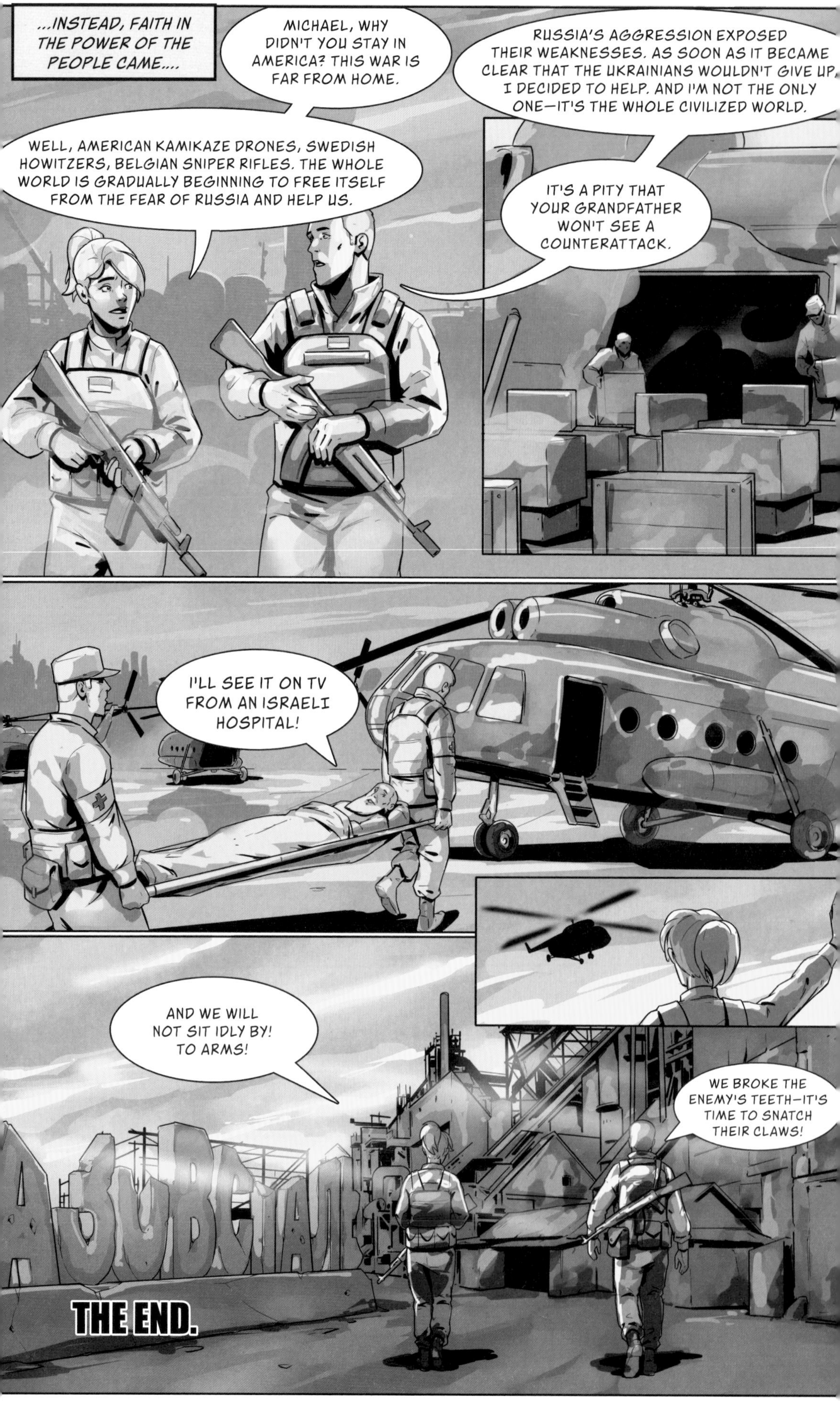

...INSTEAD, FAITH IN THE POWER OF THE PEOPLE CAME....
MICHAEL, WHY DIDN'T YOU STAY IN AMERICA? THIS WAR IS FAR FROM HOME.
WELL, AMERICAN KAMIKAZE DRONES, SWEDISH HOWITZERS, BELGIAN SNIPER RIFLES. THE WHOLE WORLD IS GRADUALLY BEGINNING TO FREE ITSELF FROM THE FEAR OF RUSSIA AND HELP US.
RUSSIA'S AGGRESSION EXPOSED THEIR WEAKNESSES. AS SOON AS IT BECAME CLEAR THAT THE UKRAINIANS WOULDN'T GIVE UP, I DECIDED TO HELP. AND I'M NOT THE ONLY ONE—IT'S THE WHOLE CIVILIZED WORLD.
IT'S A PITY THAT YOUR GRANDFATHER WON'T SEE A COUNTERATTACK.
I'LL SEE IT ON TV FROM AN ISRAELI HOSPITAL!
AND WE WILL NOT SIT IDLY BY! TO ARMS!
WE BROKE THE ENEMY'S TEETH—IT'S TIME TO SNATCH THEIR CLAWS!
THE END.

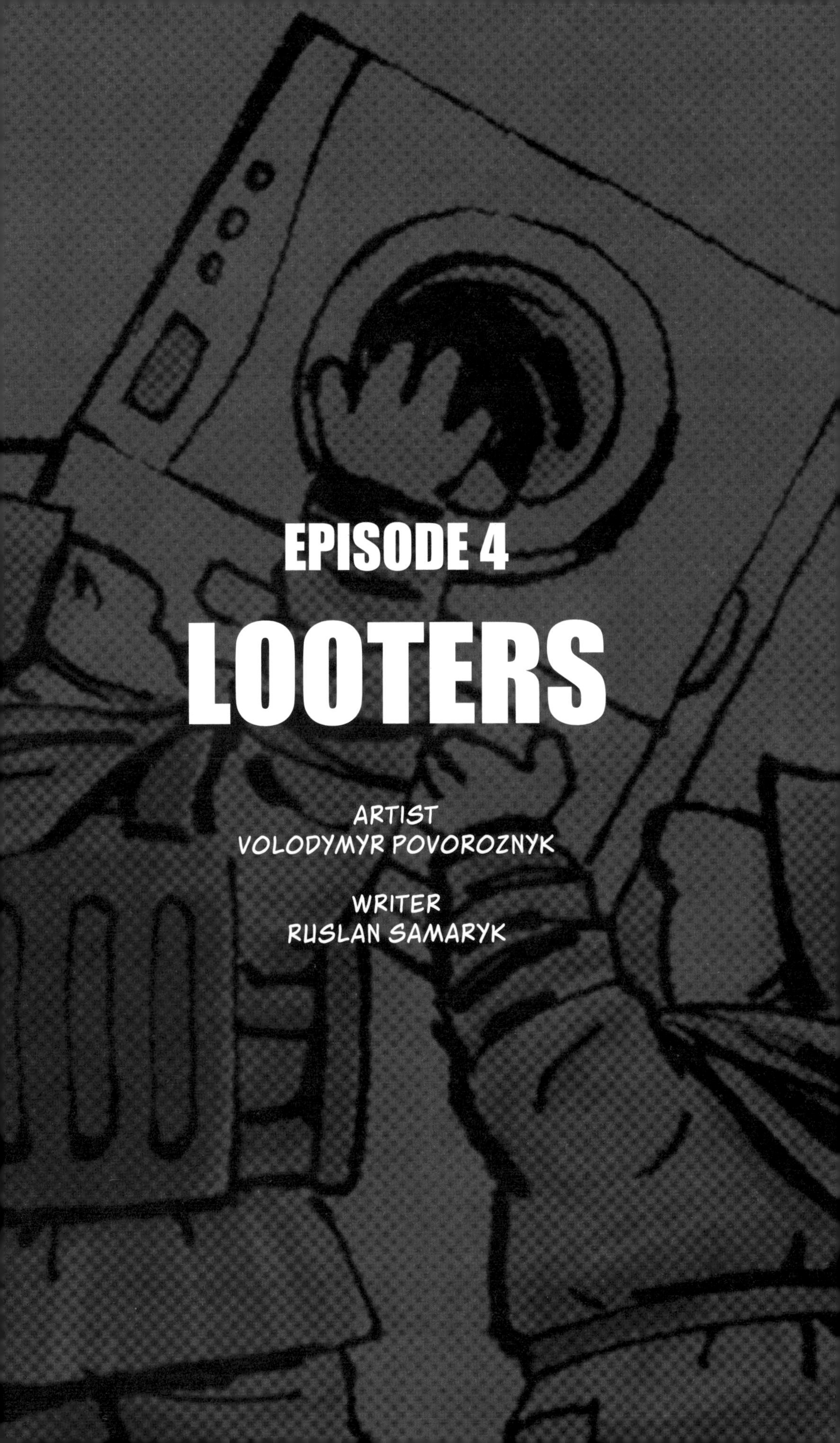

EPISODE 4
LOOTERS

ARTIST
VOLODYMYR POVOROZNYK

WRITER
RUSLAN SAMARYK

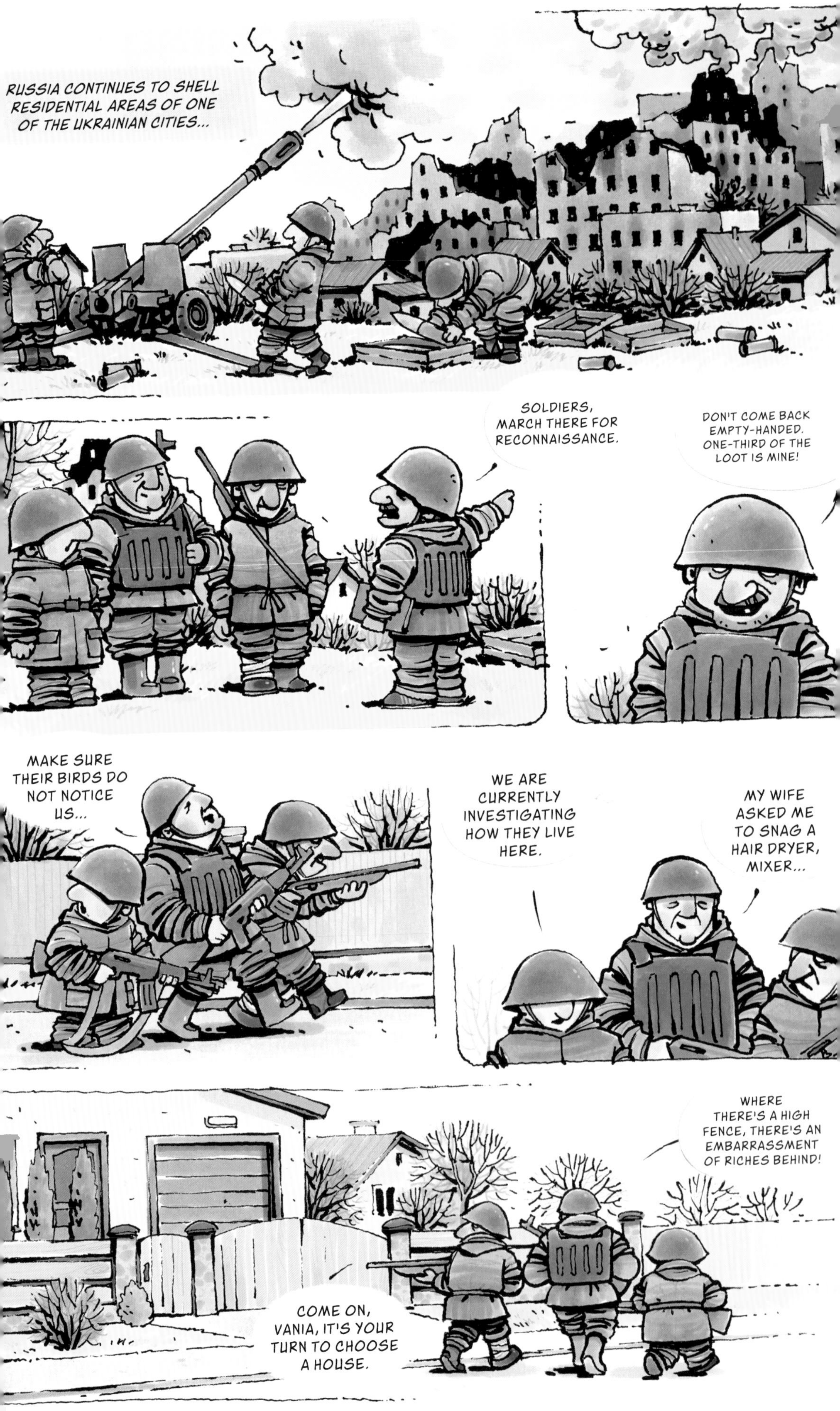
RUSSIA CONTINUES TO SHELL RESIDENTIAL AREAS OF ONE OF THE UKRAINIAN CITIES...
SOLDIERS, MARCH THERE FOR RECONNAISSANCE.
DON'T COME BACK EMPTY-HANDED. ONE-THIRD OF THE LOOT IS MINE!
MAKE SURE THEIR BIRDS DO NOT NOTICE US...
WE ARE CURRENTLY INVESTIGATING HOW THEY LIVE HERE.
MY WIFE ASKED ME TO SNAG A HAIR DRYER, MIXER...
WHERE THERE'S A HIGH FENCE, THERE'S AN EMBARRASSMENT OF RICHES BEHIND!
COME ON, VANIA, IT'S YOUR TURN TO CHOOSE A HOUSE.

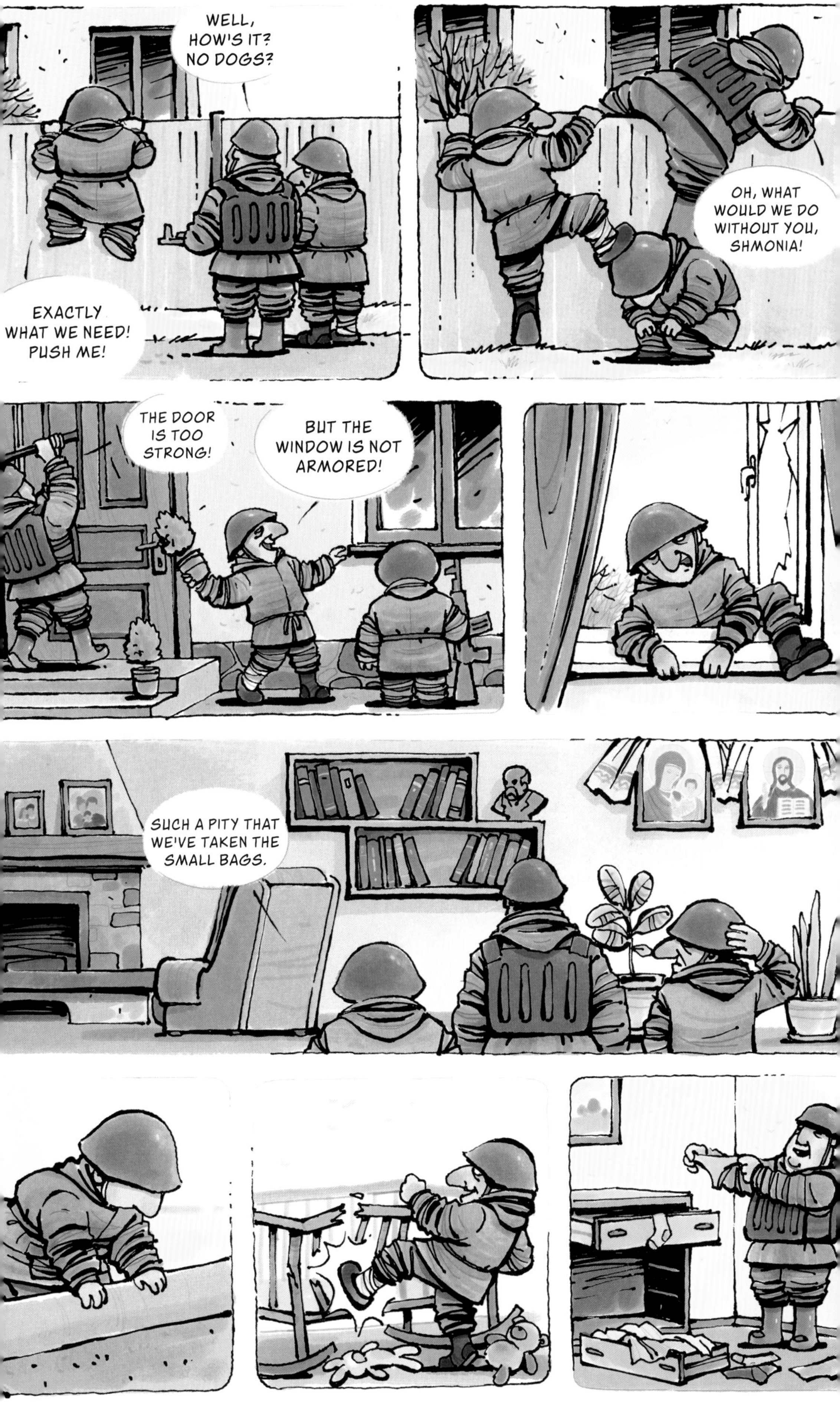
WELL, HOW'S IT? NO DOGS?
EXACTLY WHAT WE NEED! PUSH ME!
OH, WHAT WOULD WE DO WITHOUT YOU, SHMONIA!
THE DOOR IS TOO STRONG!
BUT THE WINDOW IS NOT ARMORED!
SUCH A PITY THAT WE'VE TAKEN THE SMALL BAGS.

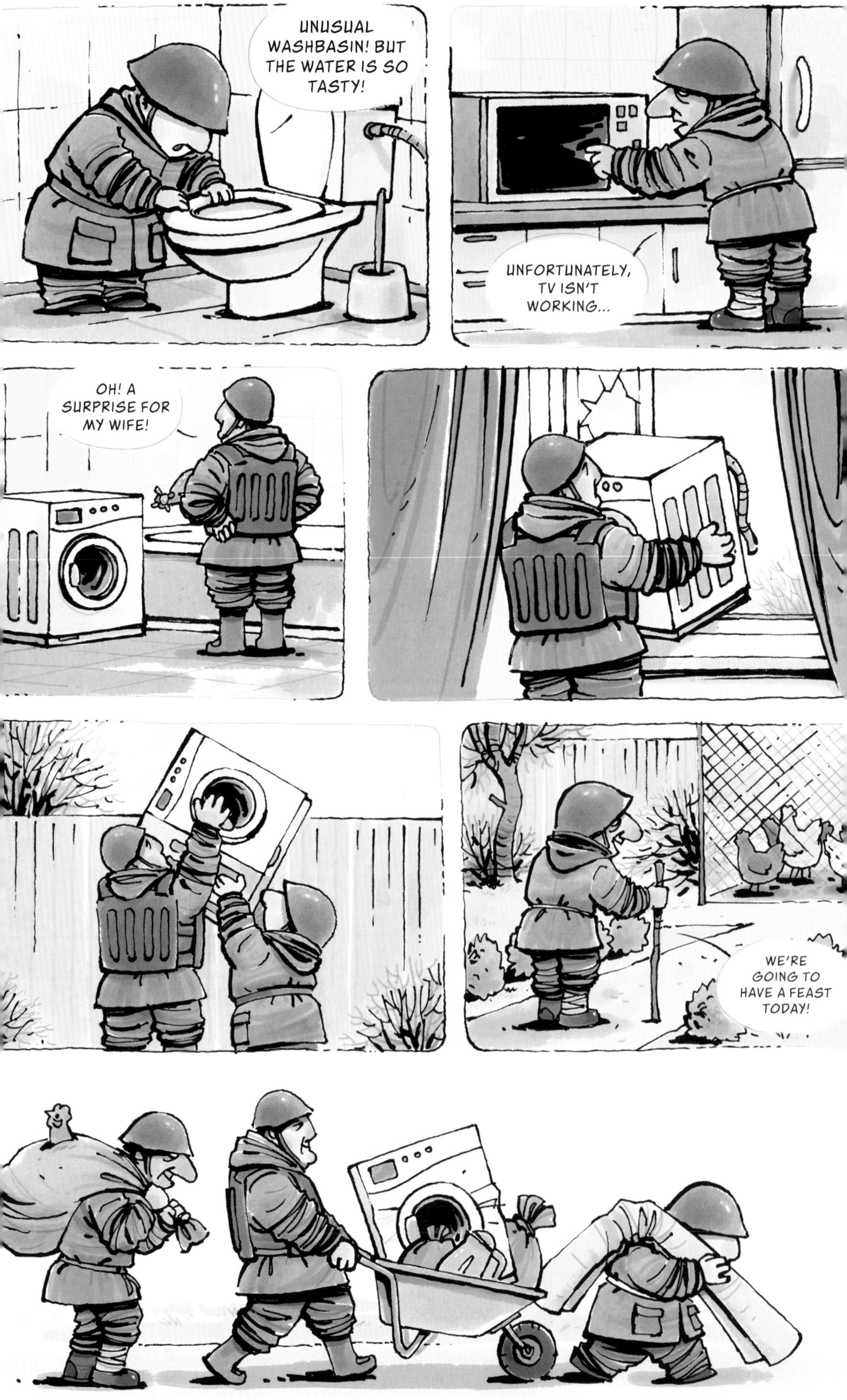
UNUSUAL WASHBASIN! BUT THE WATER IS SO TASTY!
UNFORTUNATELY, TV ISN'T WORKING...
OH! A SURPRISE FOR MY WIFE!
WE'RE GOING TO HAVE A FEAST TODAY!

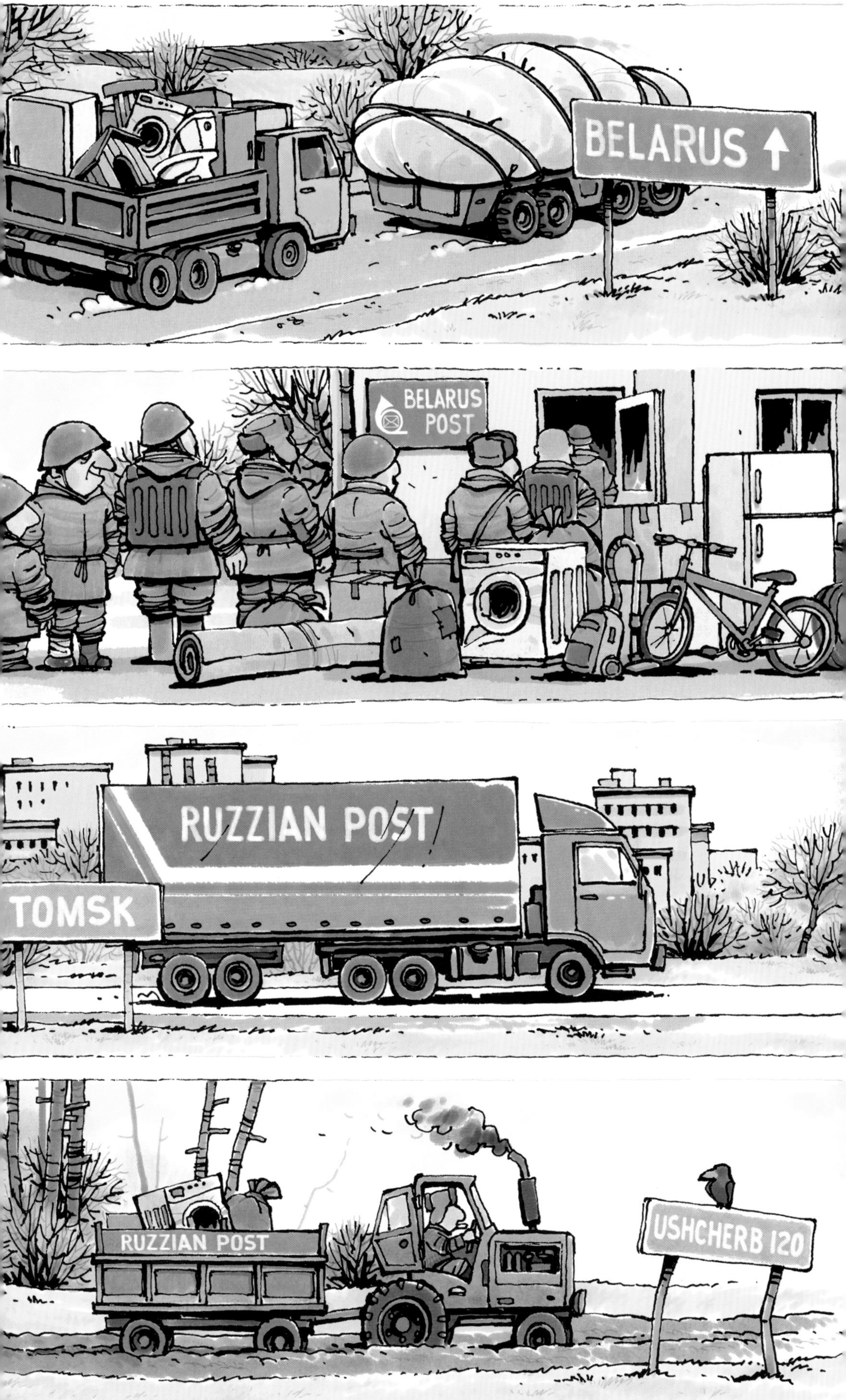
BELARUS
BELARUS POST
RUZZIAN POST
TOMSK
RUZZIAN POST
USHCHERB 120

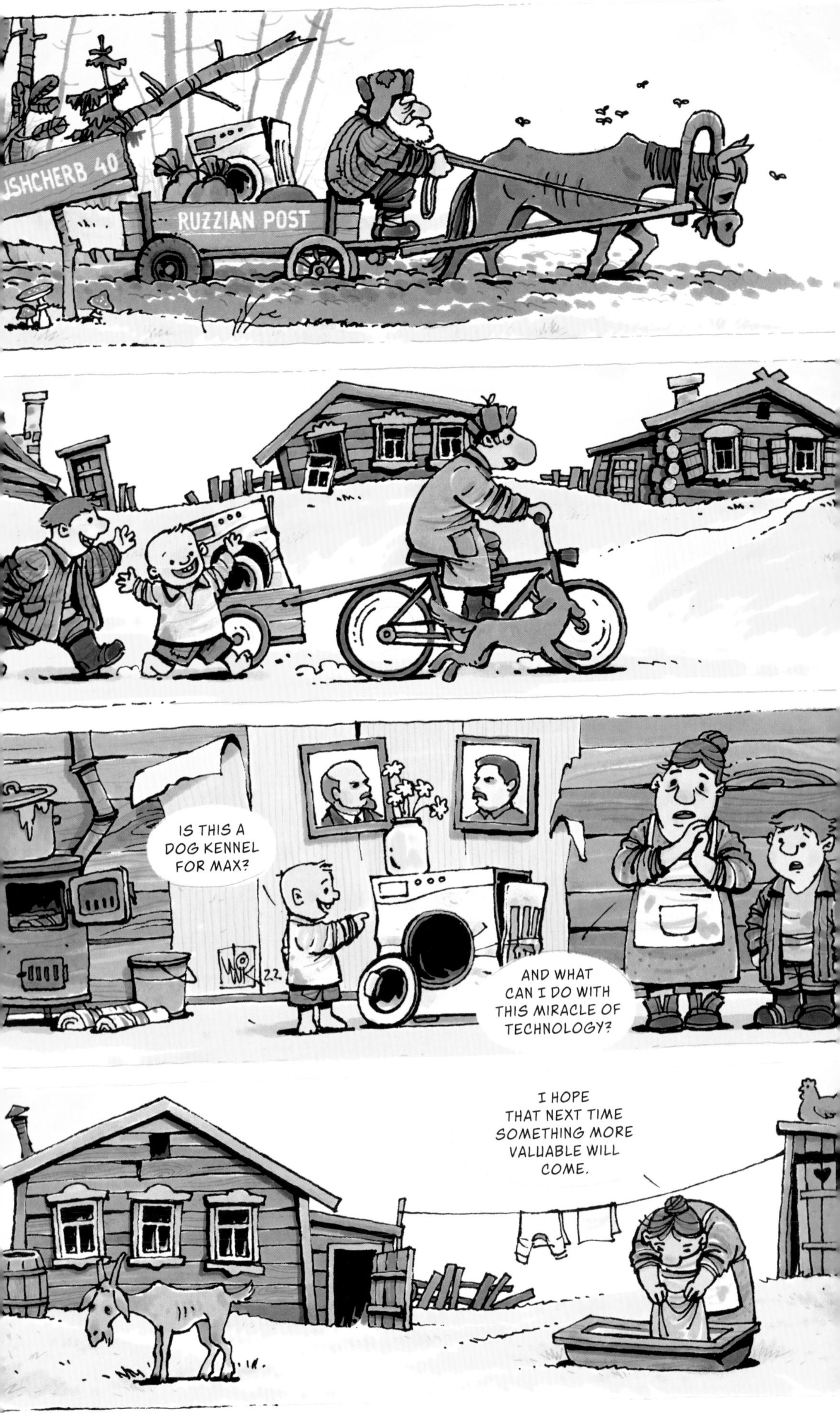

USHCHERB 40
RUZZIAN POST
IS THIS A DOG KENNEL FOR MAX?
AND WHAT CAN I DO WITH THIS MIRACLE OF TECHNOLOGY?
I HOPE THAT NEXT TIME SOMETHING MORE VALUABLE WILL COME.

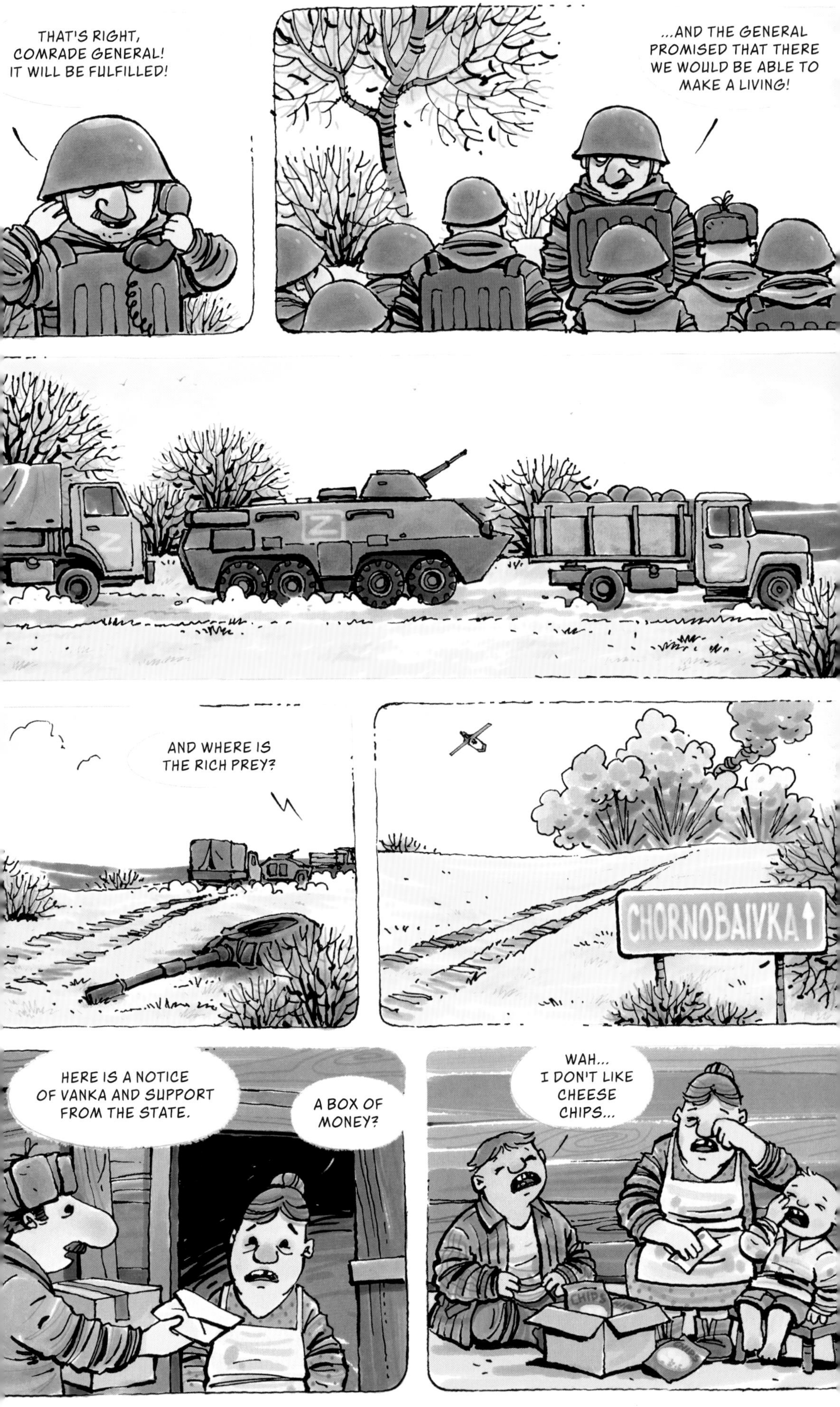
THAT'S RIGHT, COMRADE GENERAL! IT WILL BE FULFILLED!
...AND THE GENERAL PROMISED THAT THERE WE WOULD BE ABLE TO MAKE A LIVING!
Z
AND WHERE IS THE RICH PREY?
CHORNOBAIVKA
HERE IS A NOTICE OF VANKA AND SUPPORT FROM THE STATE.
A BOX OF MONEY?
WAH... I DON'T LIKE CHEESE CHIPS...
CHIPS

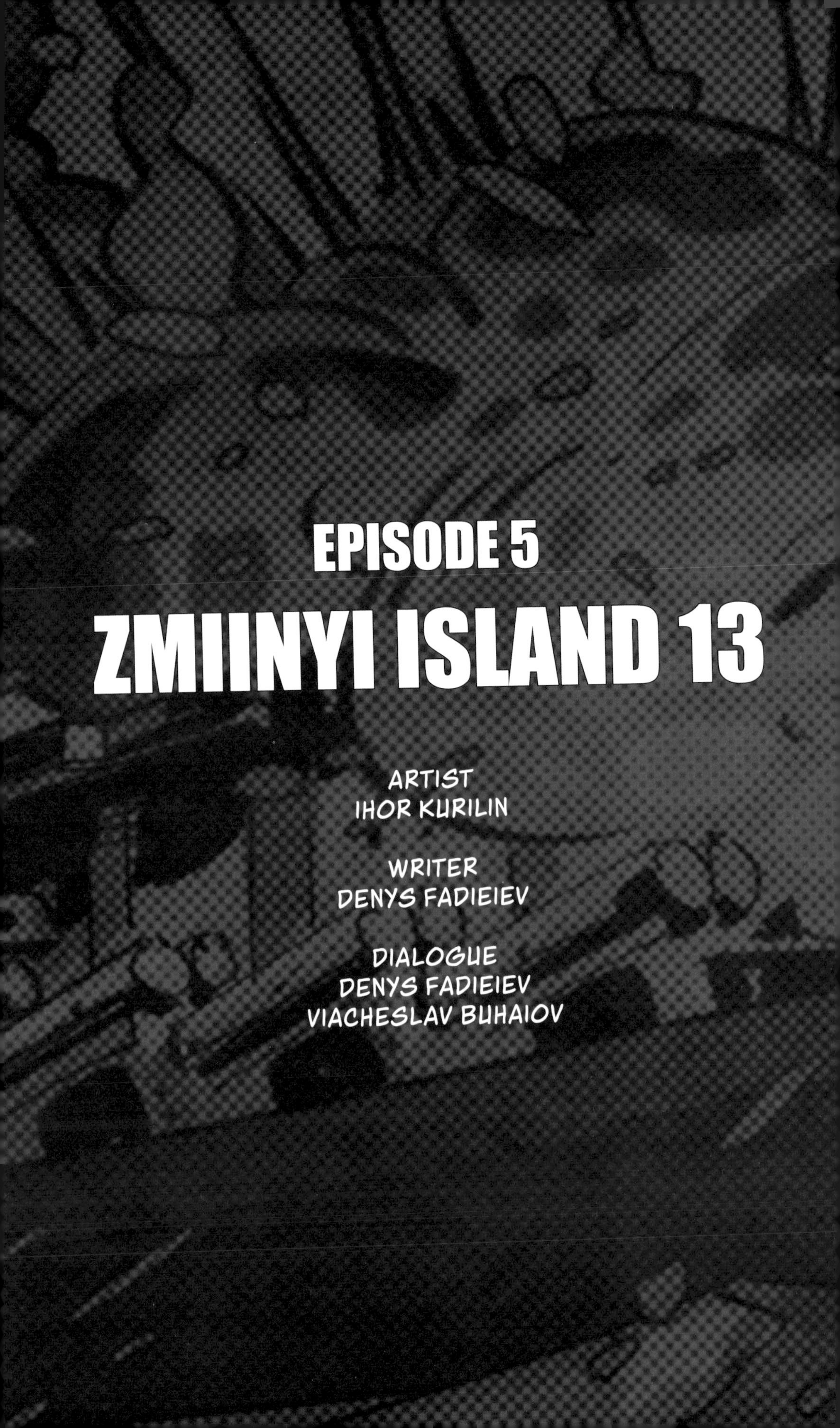

EPISODE 5
ZMIINYI ISLAND 13

ARTIST
IHOR KURILIN

WRITER
DENYS FADIEIEV

DIALOGUE
DENYS FADIEIEV
VIACHESLAV BUHAIOV

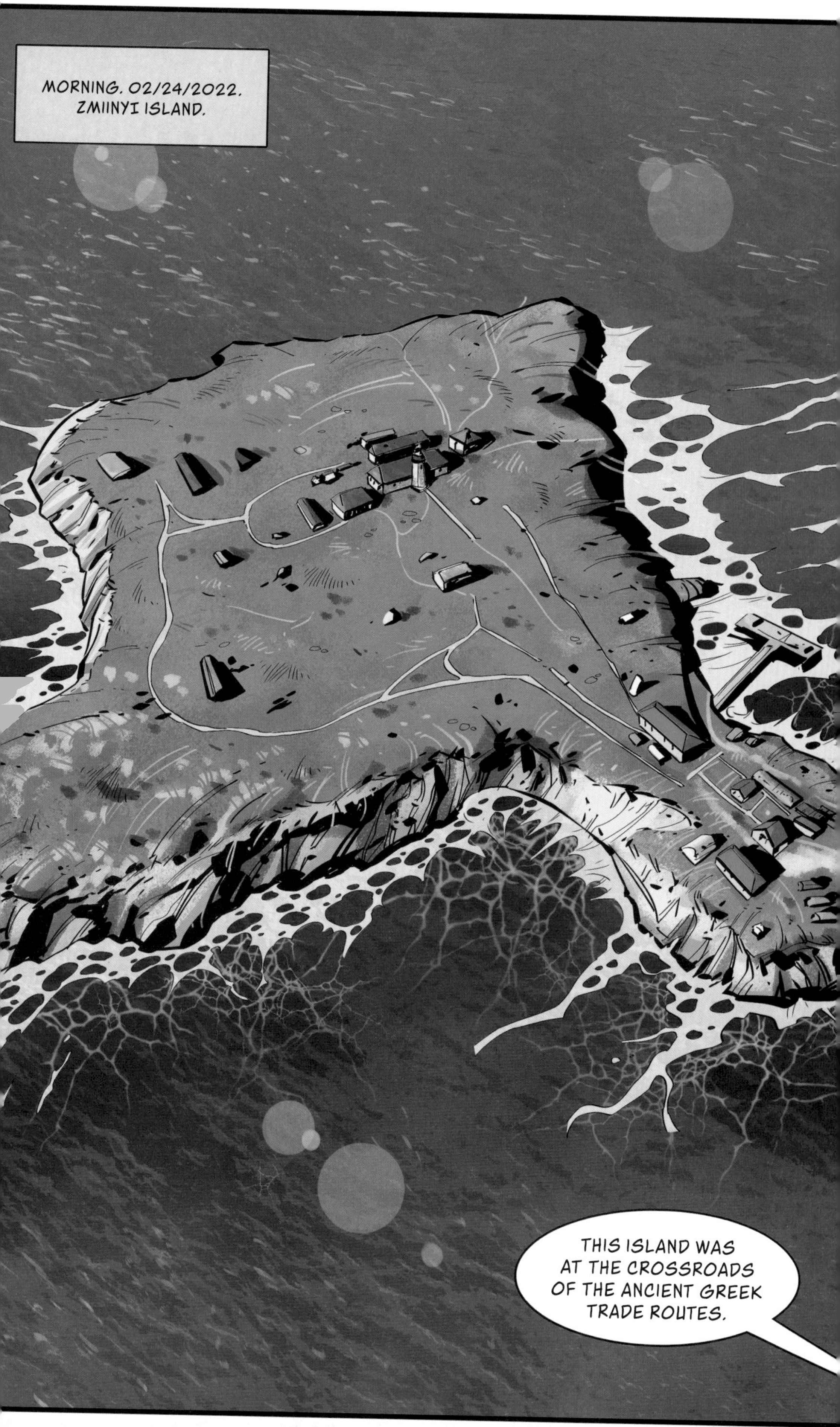
MORNING. 02/24/2022.
ZMIINYI ISLAND.
THIS ISLAND WAS AT THE CROSSROADS OF THE ANCIENT GREEK TRADE ROUTES.

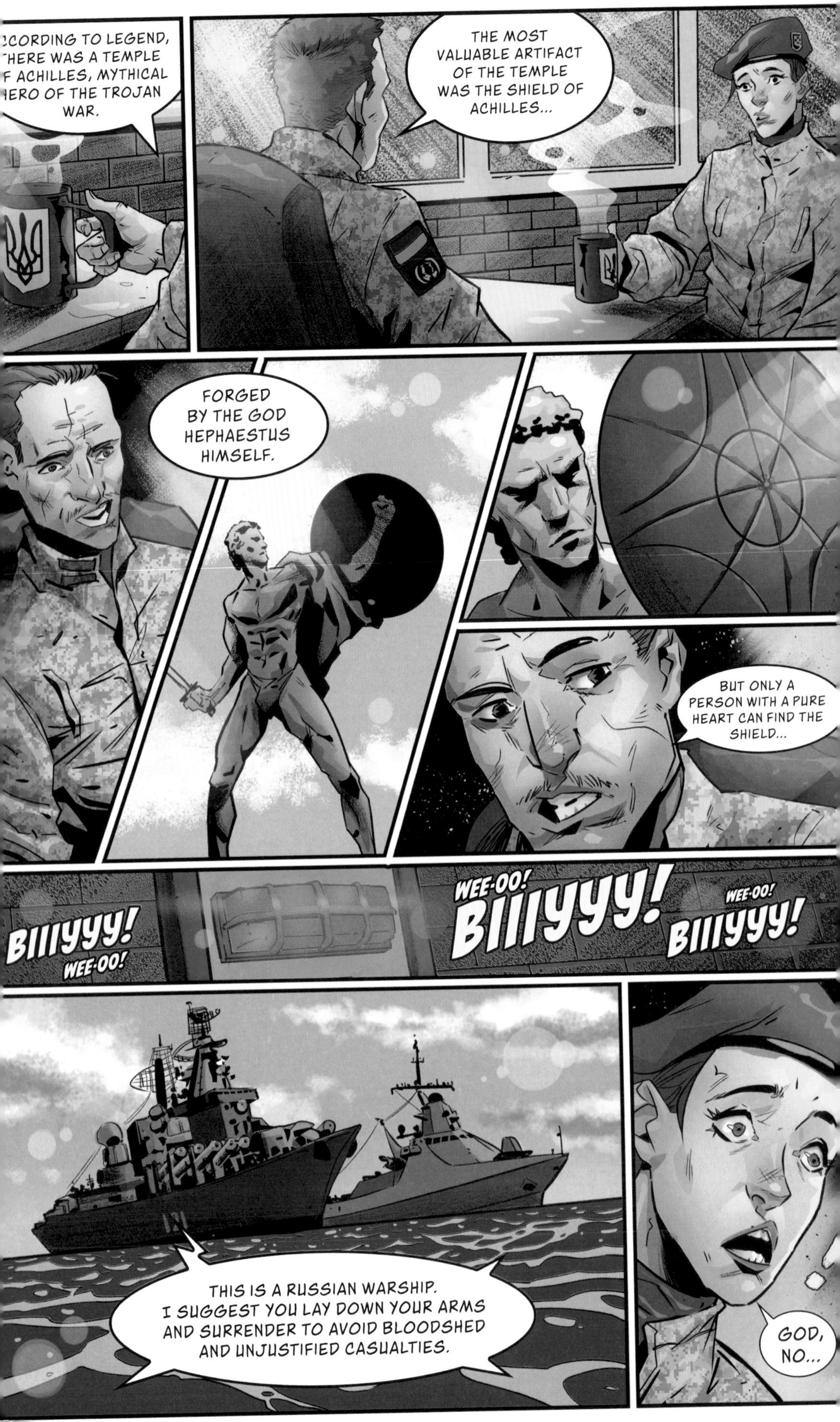
CCORDING TO LEGEND, THERE WAS A TEMPLE F ACHILLES, MYTHICAL HERO OF THE TROJAN WAR.
THE MOST VALUABLE ARTIFACT OF THE TEMPLE WAS THE SHIELD OF ACHILLES...
FORGED BY THE GOD HEPHAESTUS HIMSELF.
BUT ONLY A PERSON WITH A PURE HEART CAN FIND THE SHIELD...
BIIIYYY! WEE-OO!
WEE-OO! BIIIYYY!
WEE-OO! BIIIYYY!
THIS IS A RUSSIAN WARSHIP. I SUGGEST YOU LAY DOWN YOUR ARMS AND SURRENDER TO AVOID BLOODSHED AND UNJUSTIFIED CASUALTIES.
GOD, NO...

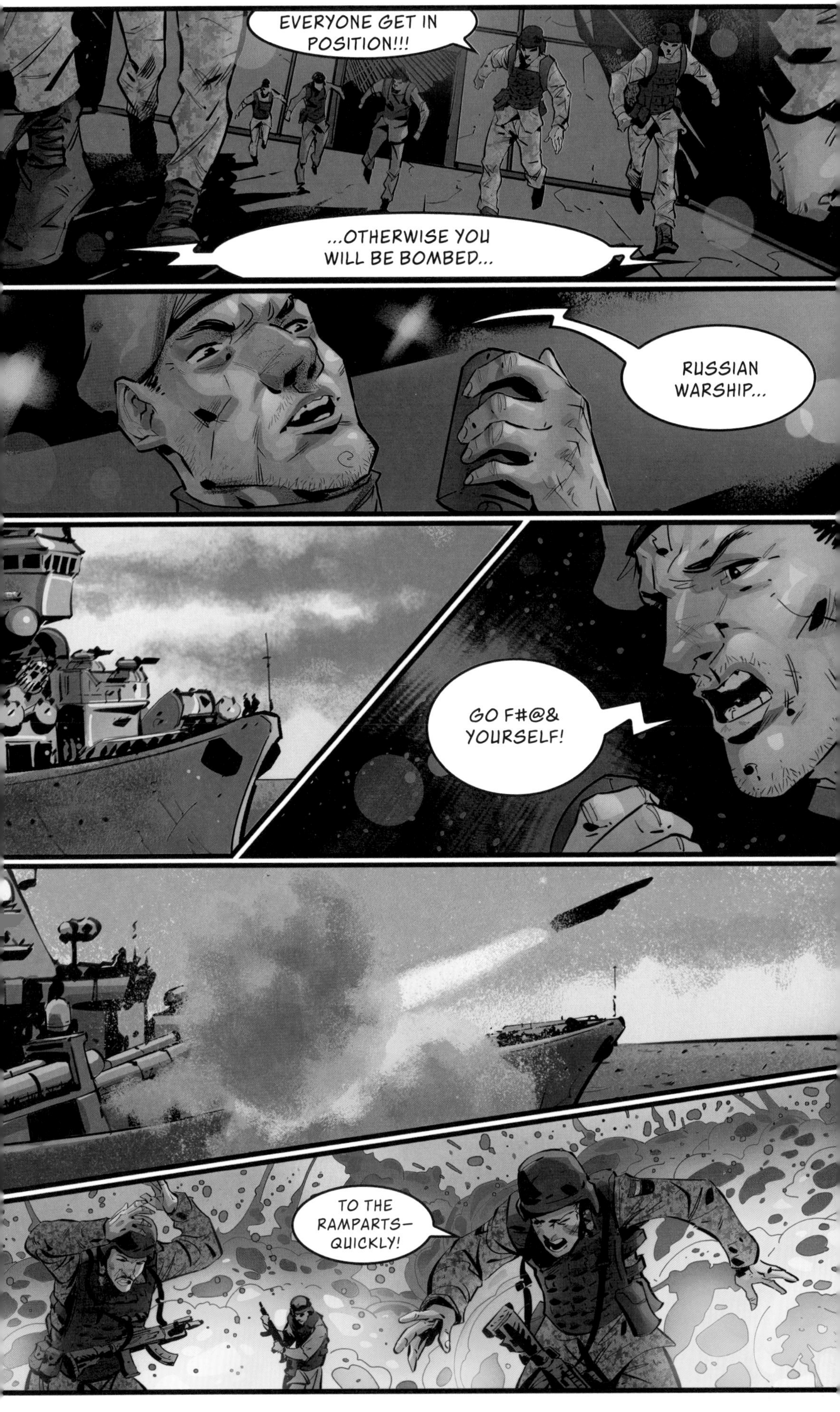
EVERYONE GET IN POSITION!!!
...OTHERWISE YOU WILL BE BOMBED...
RUSSIAN WARSHIP...
GO F#@& YOURSELF!
TO THE RAMPARTS— QUICKLY!

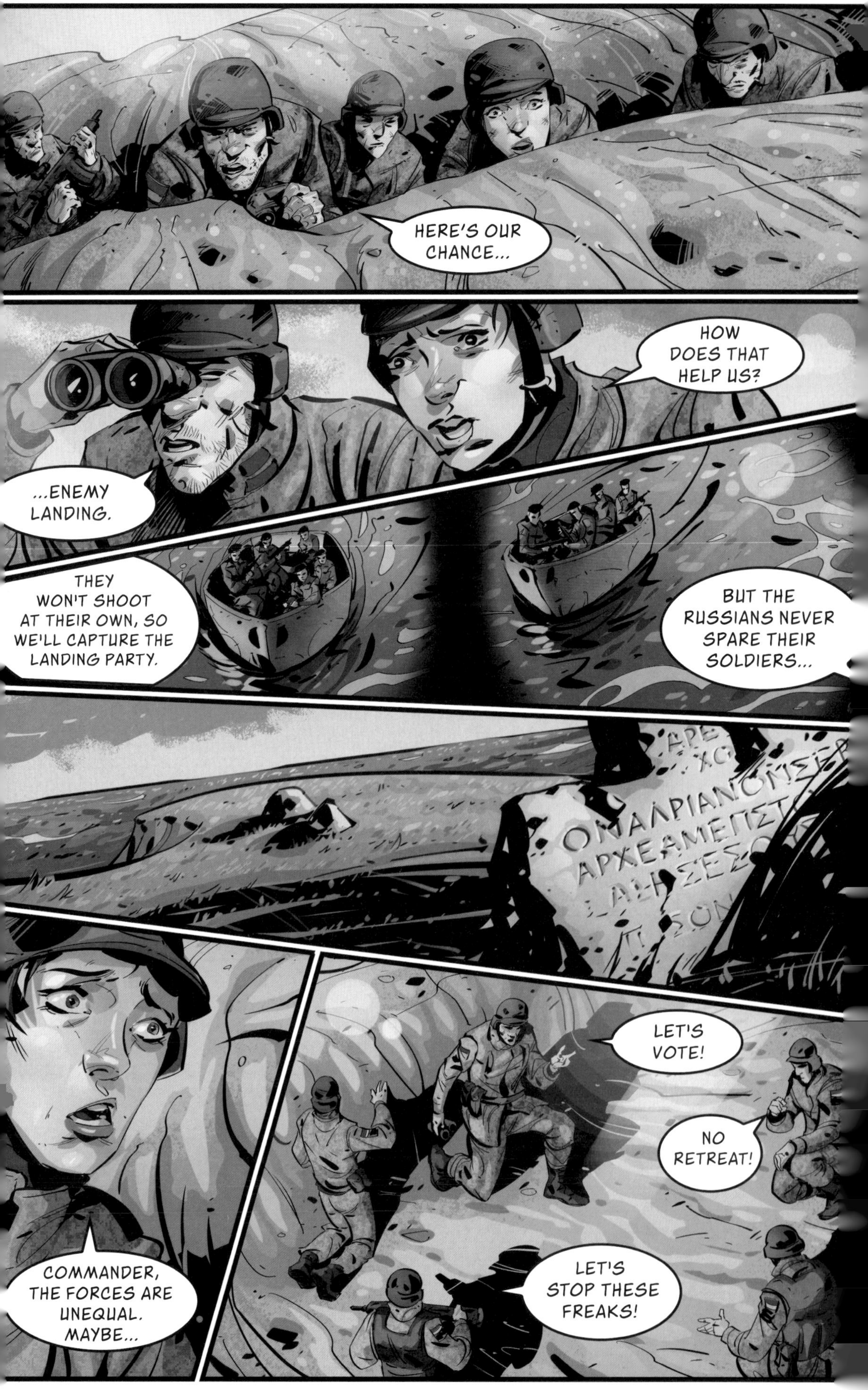
HERE'S OUR CHANCE...
HOW DOES THAT HELP US?
...ENEMY LANDING.
THEY WON'T SHOOT AT THEIR OWN, SO WE'LL CAPTURE THE LANDING PARTY.
BUT THE RUSSIANS NEVER SPARE THEIR SOLDIERS...
COMMANDER, THE FORCES ARE UNEQUAL. MAYBE...
LET'S VOTE!
NO RETREAT!
LET'S STOP THESE FREAKS!

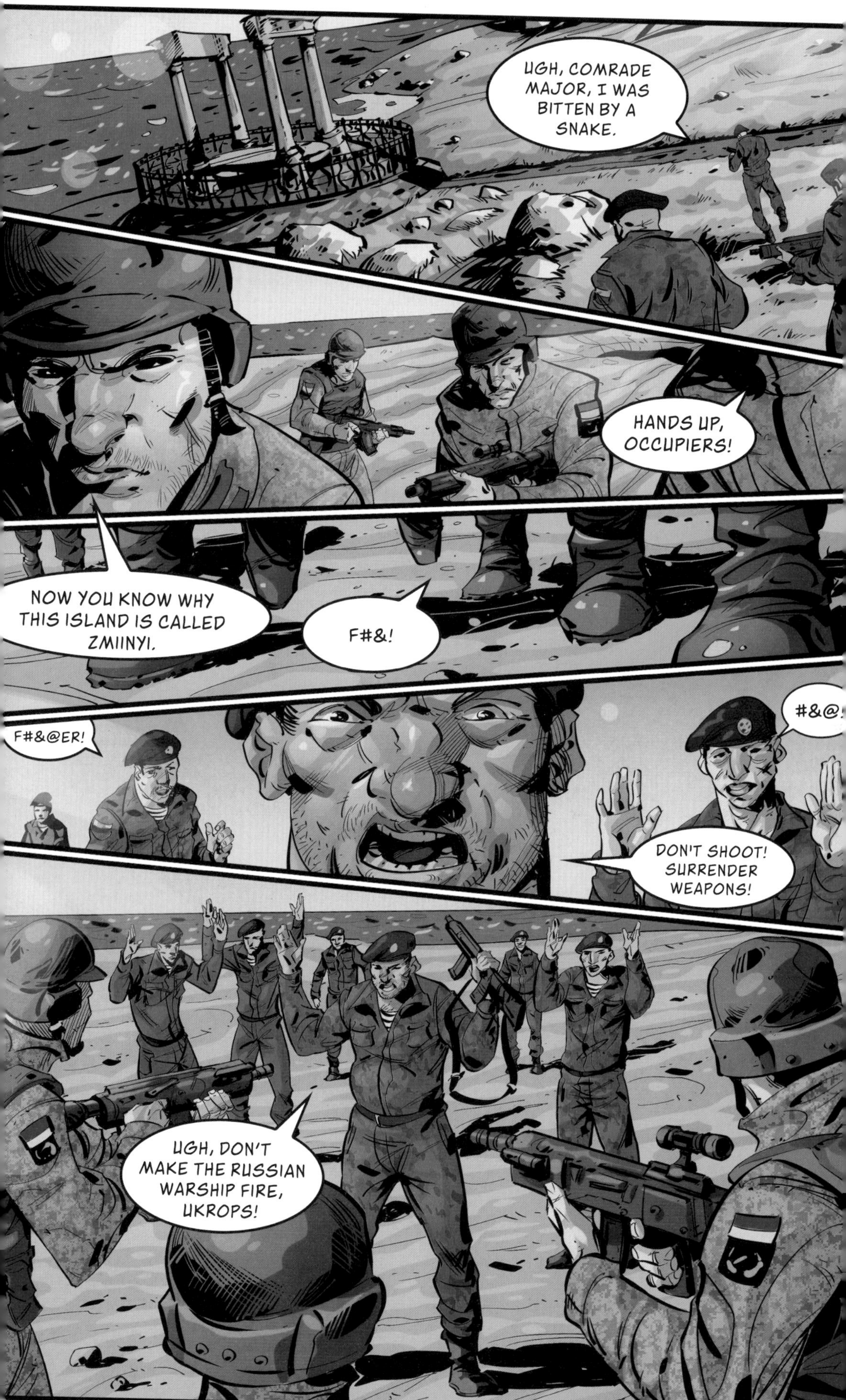
UGH, COMRADE MAJOR, I WAS BITTEN BY A SNAKE.
HANDS UP, OCCUPIERS!
NOW YOU KNOW WHY THIS ISLAND IS CALLED ZMIINYI.
F#&!
F#&@ER!
#&@!
DON'T SHOOT! SURRENDER WEAPONS!
UGH, DON'T MAKE THE RUSSIAN WARSHIP FIRE, UKROPS!

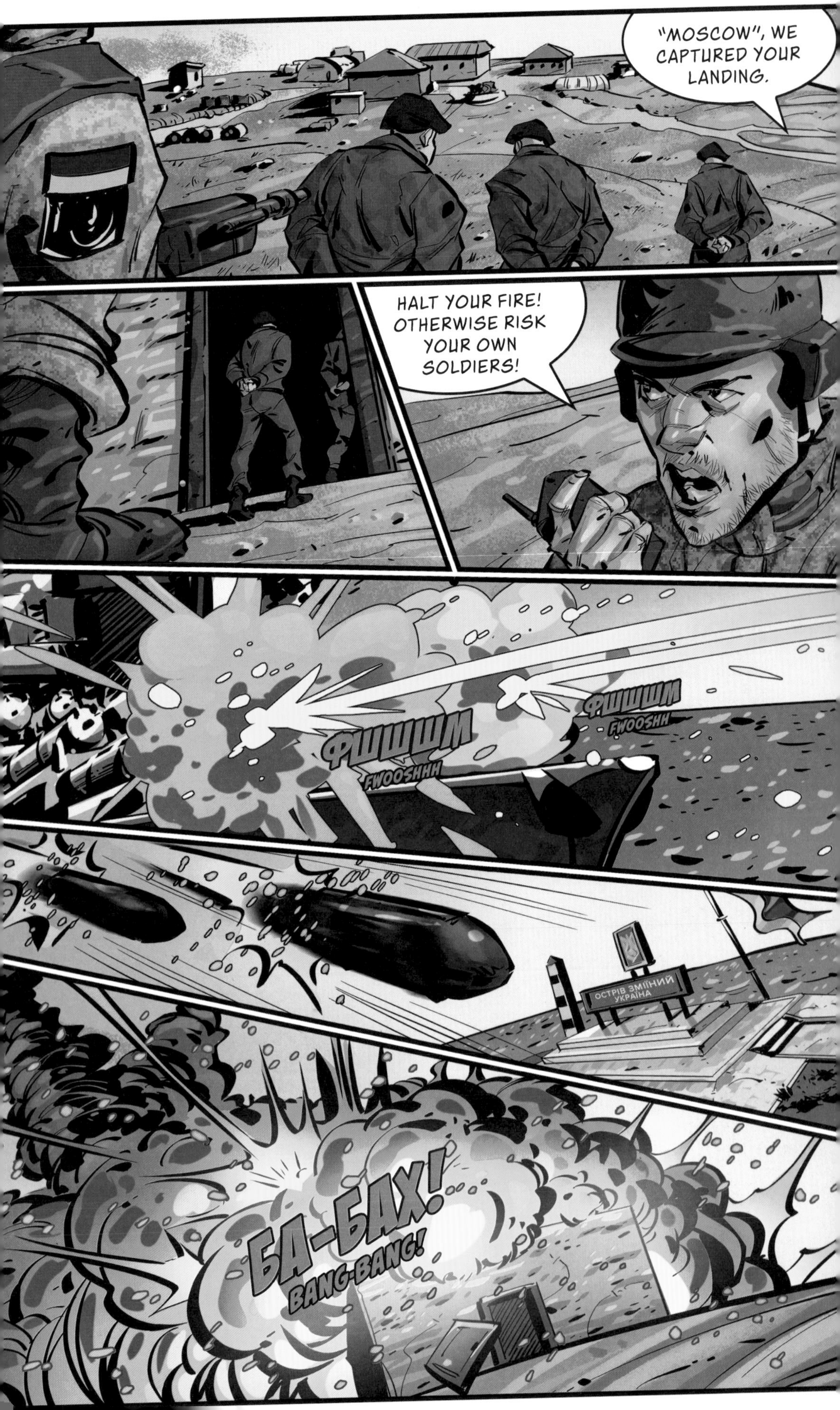
"MOSCOW", WE CAPTURED YOUR LANDING.
HALT YOUR FIRE! OTHERWISE RISK YOUR OWN SOLDIERS!
ФШШМ
FWOOSHHH
ФШШМ
FWOOSHH
ОСТРІВ ЗМІЇНИЙ
УКРАЇНА
БА-БАХ!
BANG-BANG!

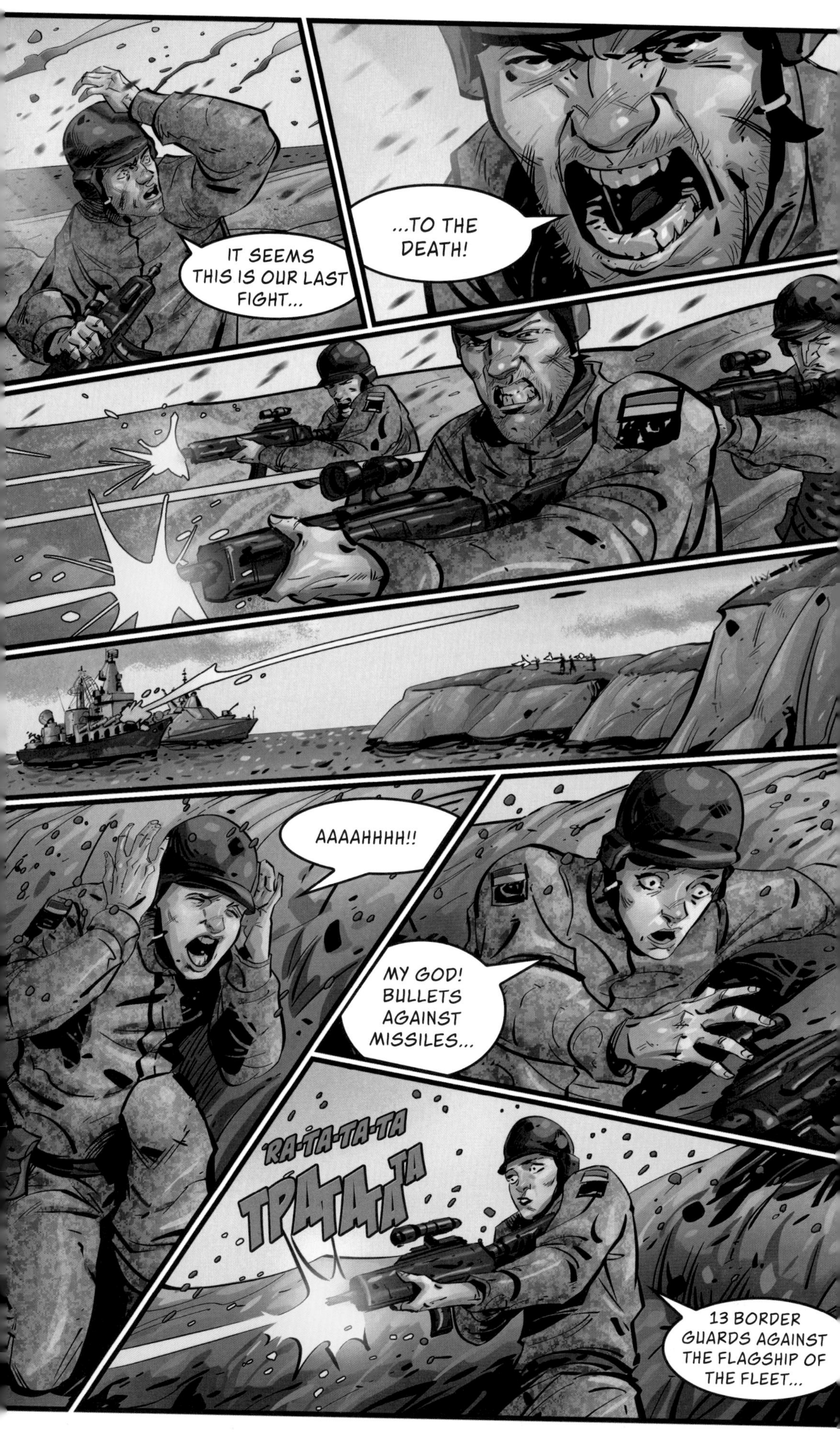
IT SEEMS THIS IS OUR LAST FIGHT...
...TO THE DEATH!
AAAAHHHH!!
MY GOD! BULLETS AGAINST MISSILES...
RA-TA-TA-TA
TPATATATA
13 BORDER GUARDS AGAINST THE FLAGSHIP OF THE FLEET...

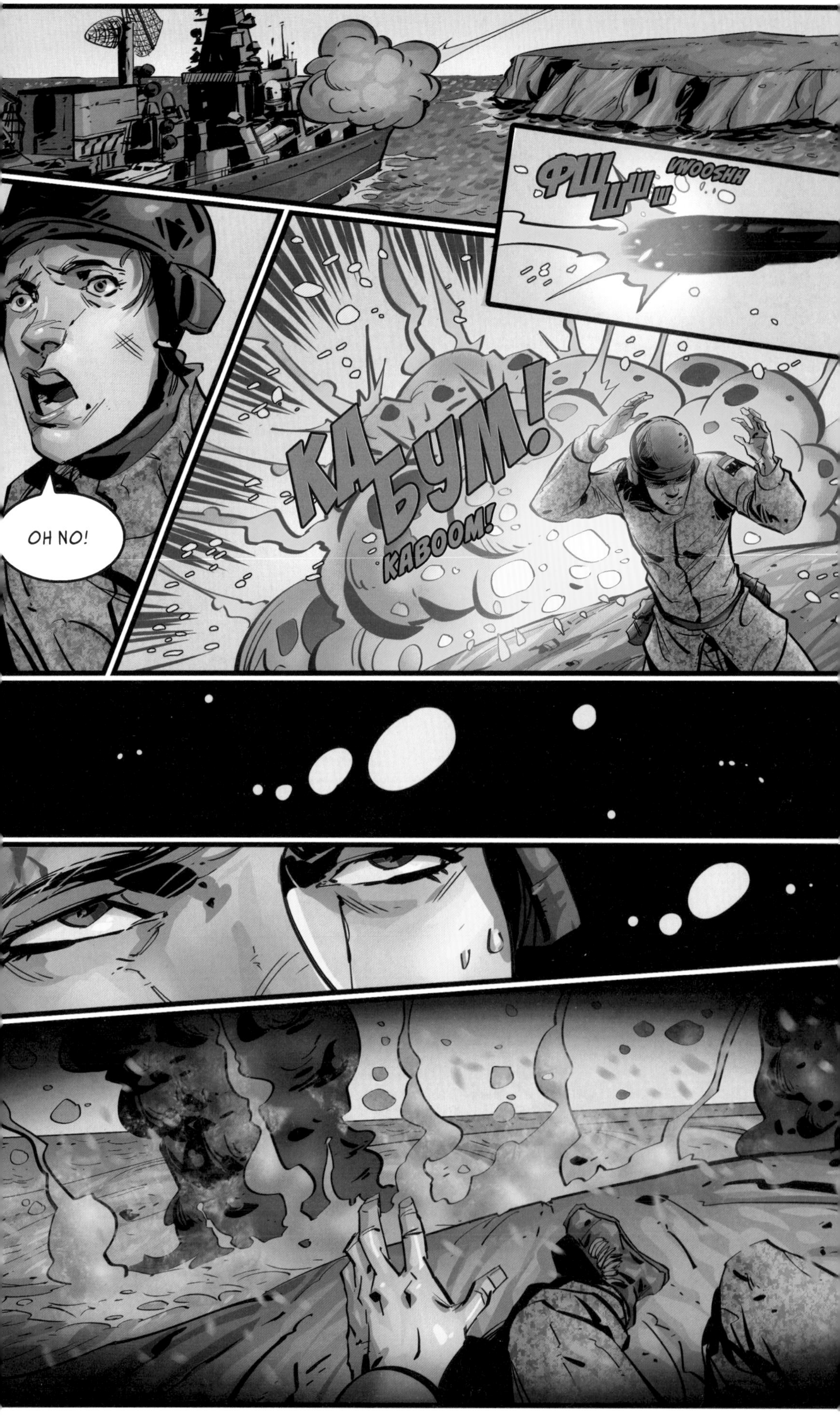
ФШШШ
WOOSHH
OH NO!
КАБУМ!
KABOOM!

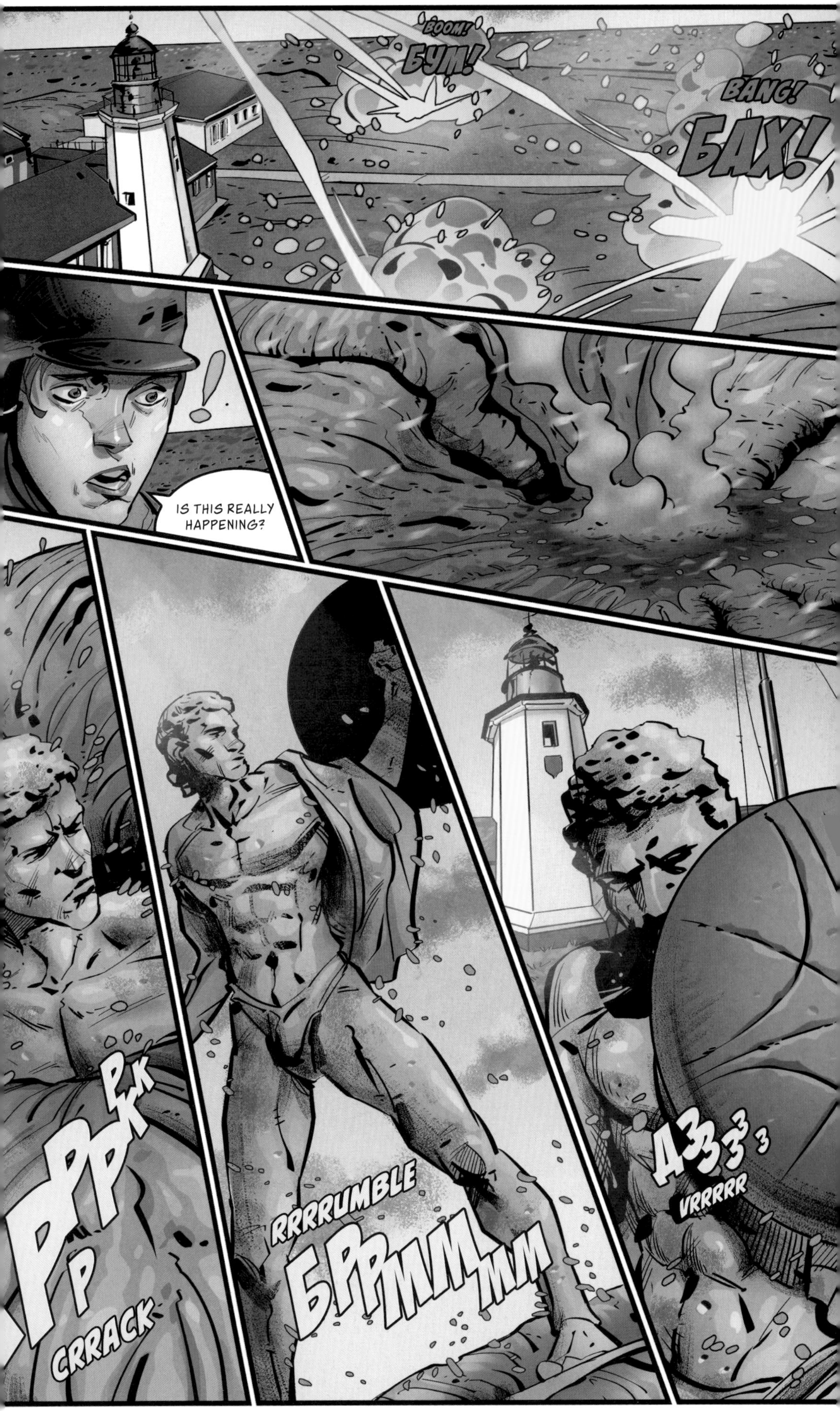

BOOM!
БУМ!
BANG!
БАХ!
IS THIS REALLY HAPPENING?
PPPPKK
CRRACK
RRRRUMBLE
БРРММММ
ДЗЗЗЗЗ
VRRRRR

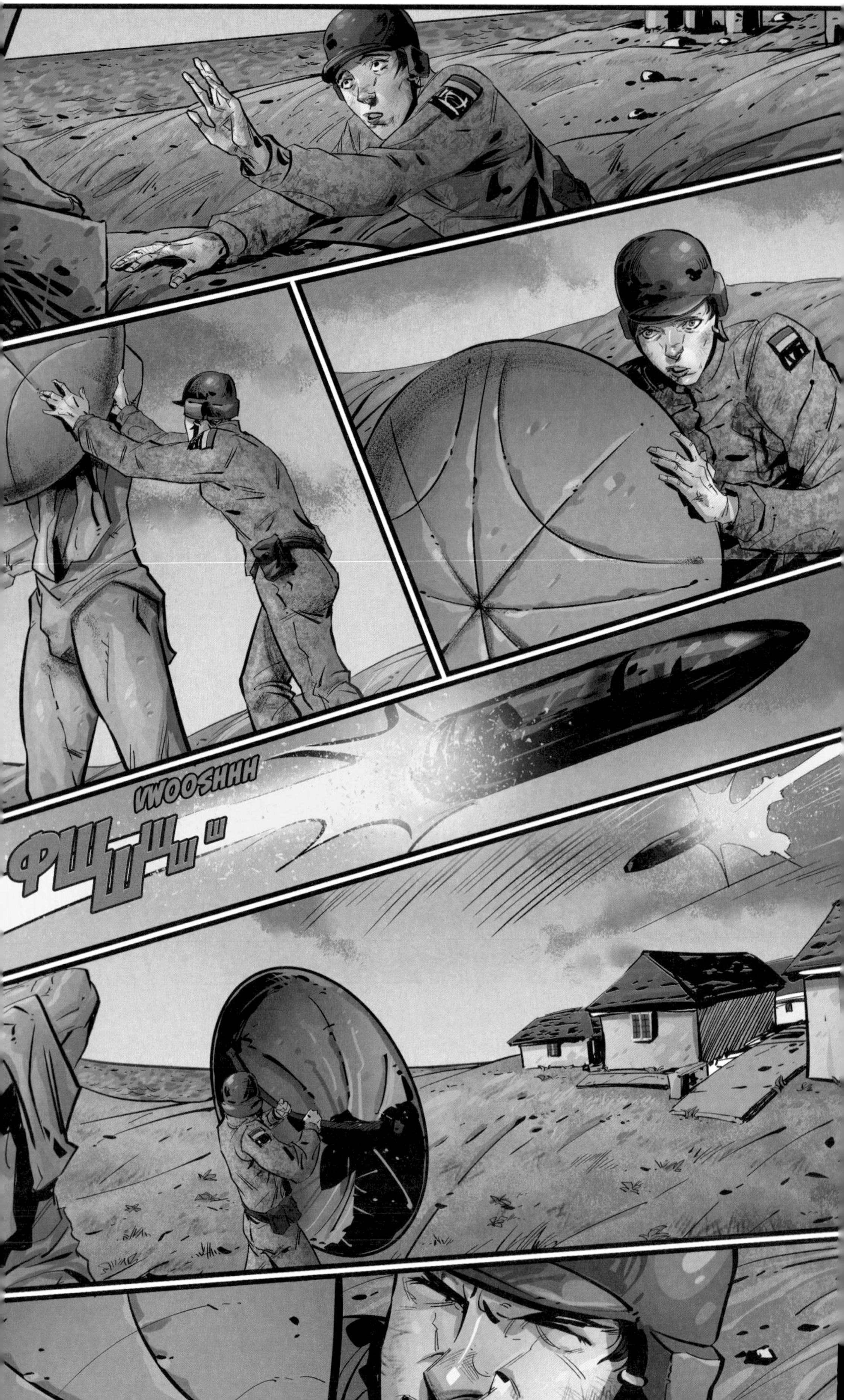
ФШШШШ
VWOOSHHH

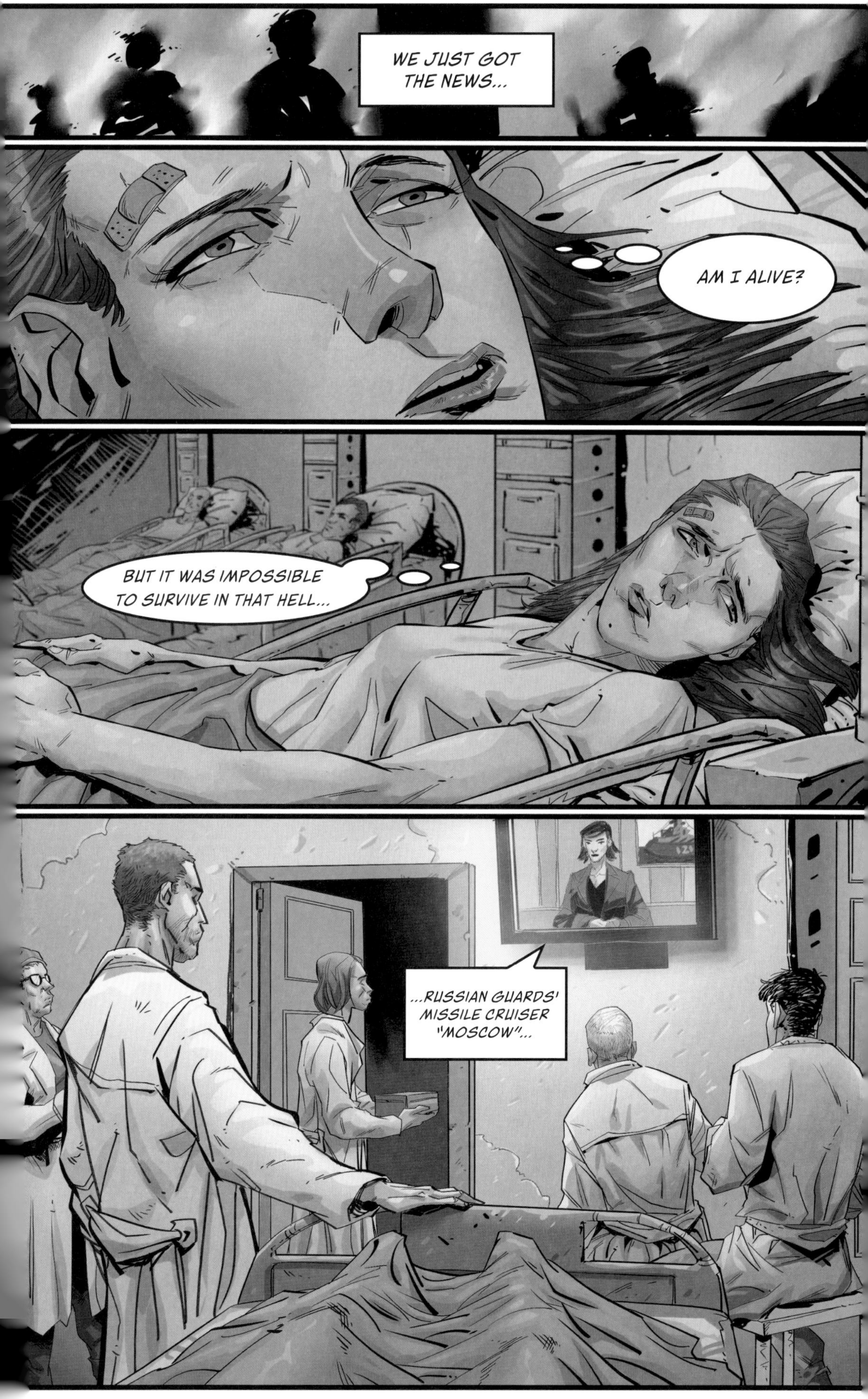
WE JUST GOT THE NEWS...
AM I ALIVE?
BUT IT WAS IMPOSSIBLE TO SURVIVE IN THAT HELL...
...RUSSIAN GUARDS' MISSILE CRUISER "MOSCOW"...

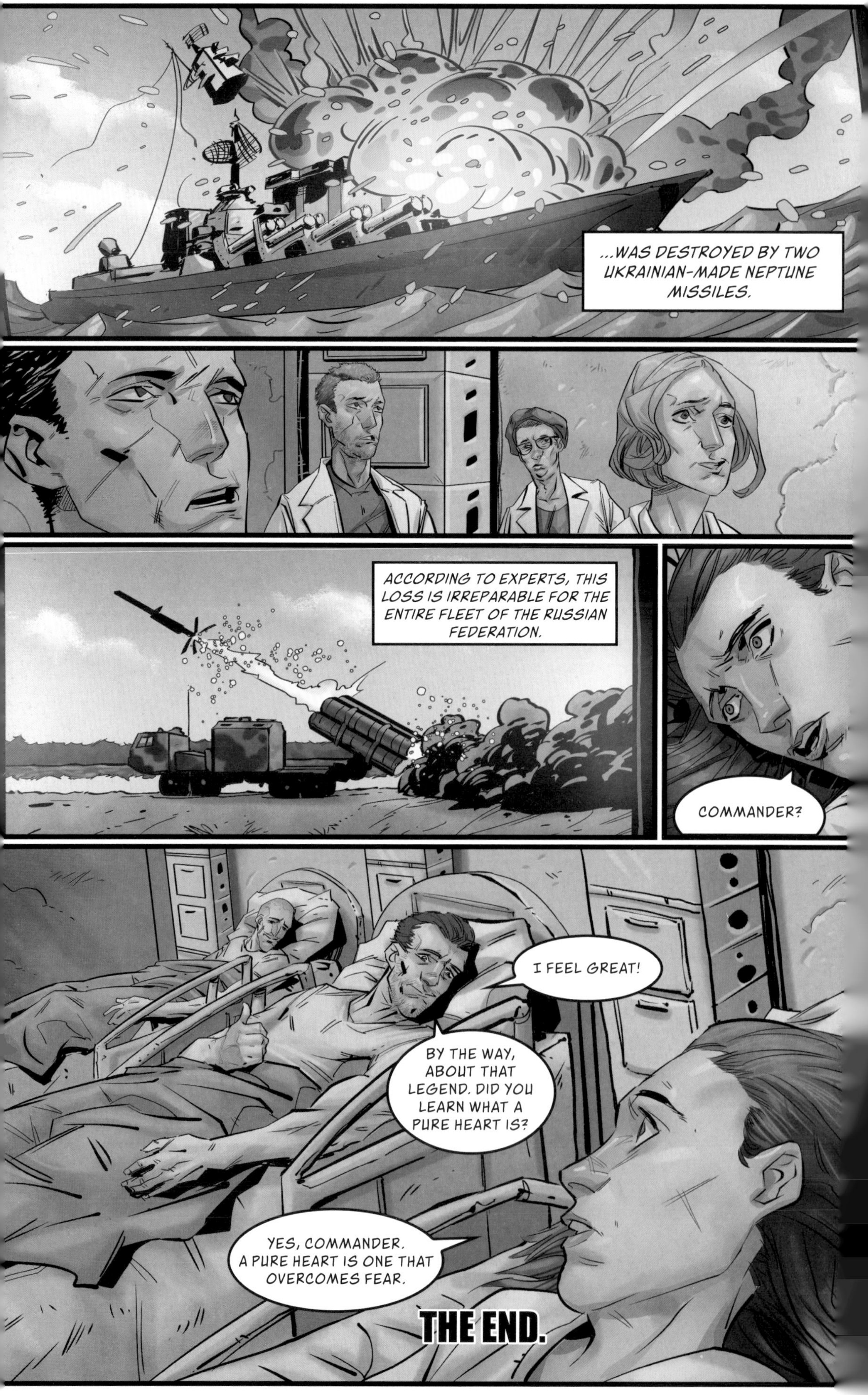
...WAS DESTROYED BY TWO UKRAINIAN-MADE NEPTUNE MISSILES.
ACCORDING TO EXPERTS, THIS LOSS IS IRREPARABLE FOR THE ENTIRE FLEET OF THE RUSSIAN FEDERATION.
COMMANDER?
I FEEL GREAT!
BY THE WAY, ABOUT THAT LEGEND. DID YOU LEARN WHAT A PURE HEART IS?
YES, COMMANDER. A PURE HEART IS ONE THAT OVERCOMES FEAR.
THE END.

EPISODE 6

THROUGHOUT THE CENTURIES

ARTIST
MAKSYM BOHDANOVSKYI

WRITER
DENYS FADIEIEV

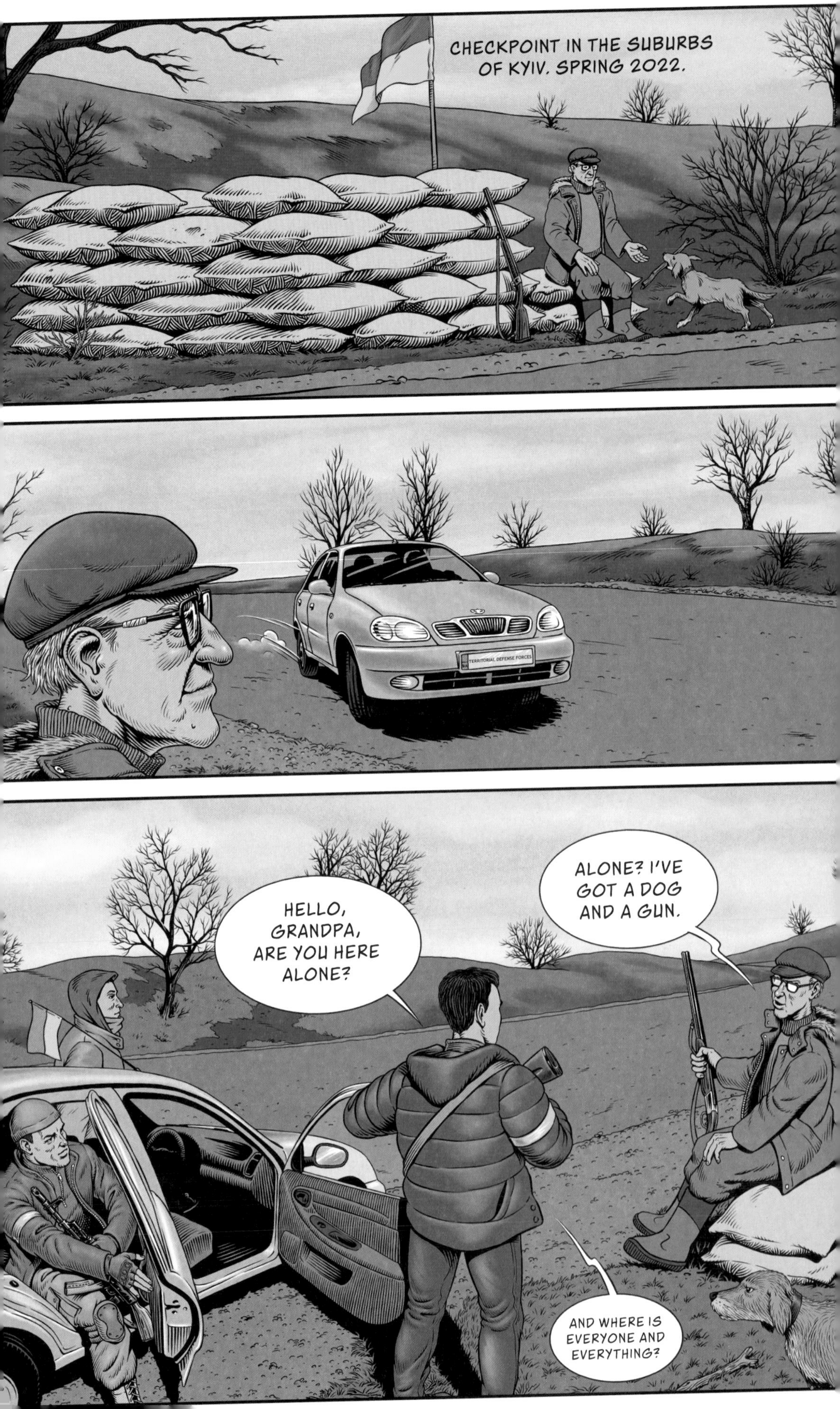
CHECKPOINT IN THE SUBURBS OF KYIV. SPRING 2022.
TERRITORIAL DEFENSE FORCES
HELLO, GRANDPA, ARE YOU HERE ALONE?
ALONE? I'VE GOT A DOG AND A GUN.
AND WHERE IS EVERYONE AND EVERYTHING?

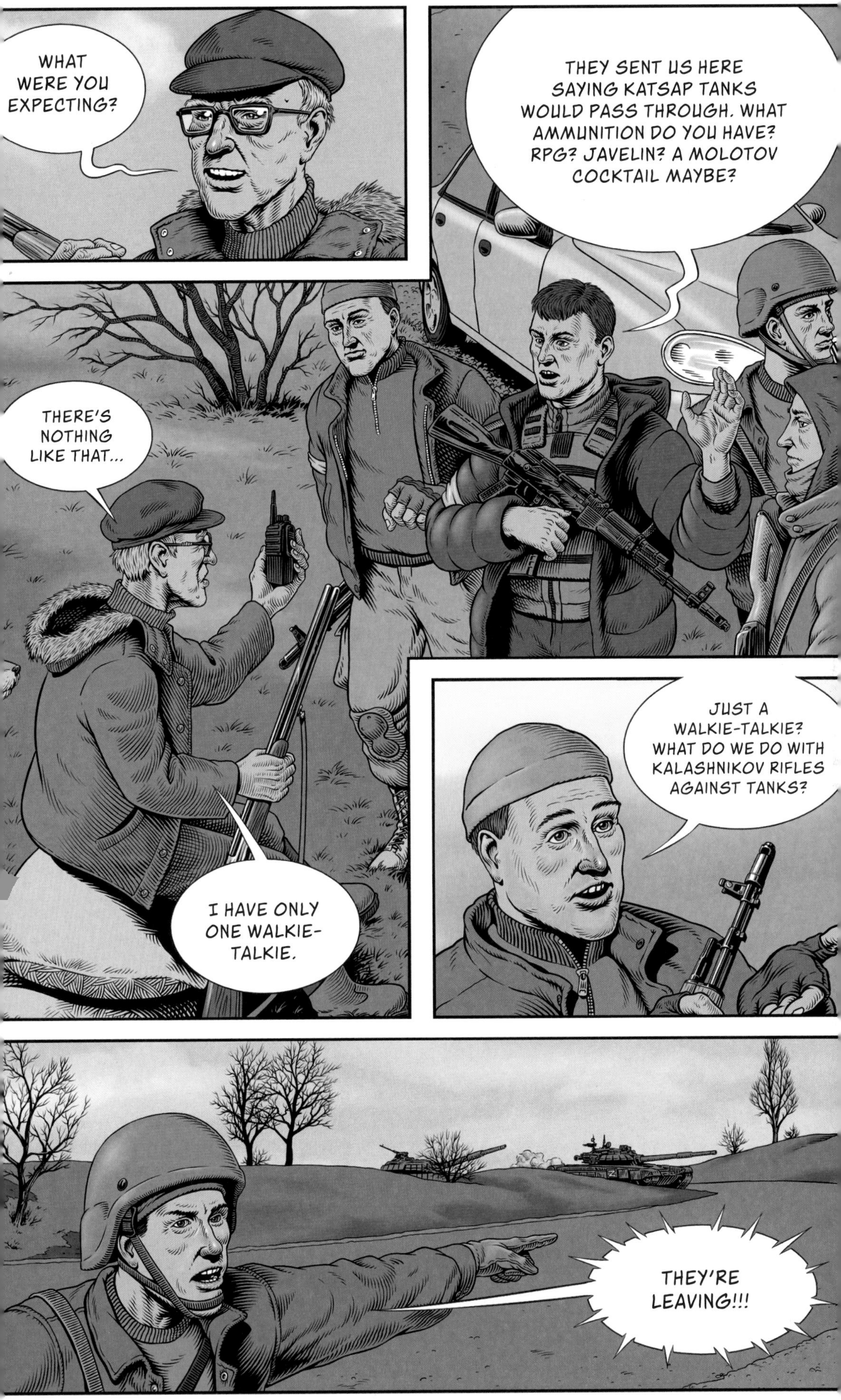
WHAT WERE YOU EXPECTING?
THEY SENT US HERE SAYING KATSAP TANKS WOULD PASS THROUGH. WHAT AMMUNITION DO YOU HAVE? RPG? JAVELIN? A MOLOTOV COCKTAIL MAYBE?
THERE'S NOTHING LIKE THAT...
I HAVE ONLY ONE WALKIE-TALKIE.
JUST A WALKIE-TALKIE? WHAT DO WE DO WITH KALASHNIKOV RIFLES AGAINST TANKS?
THEY'RE LEAVING!!!

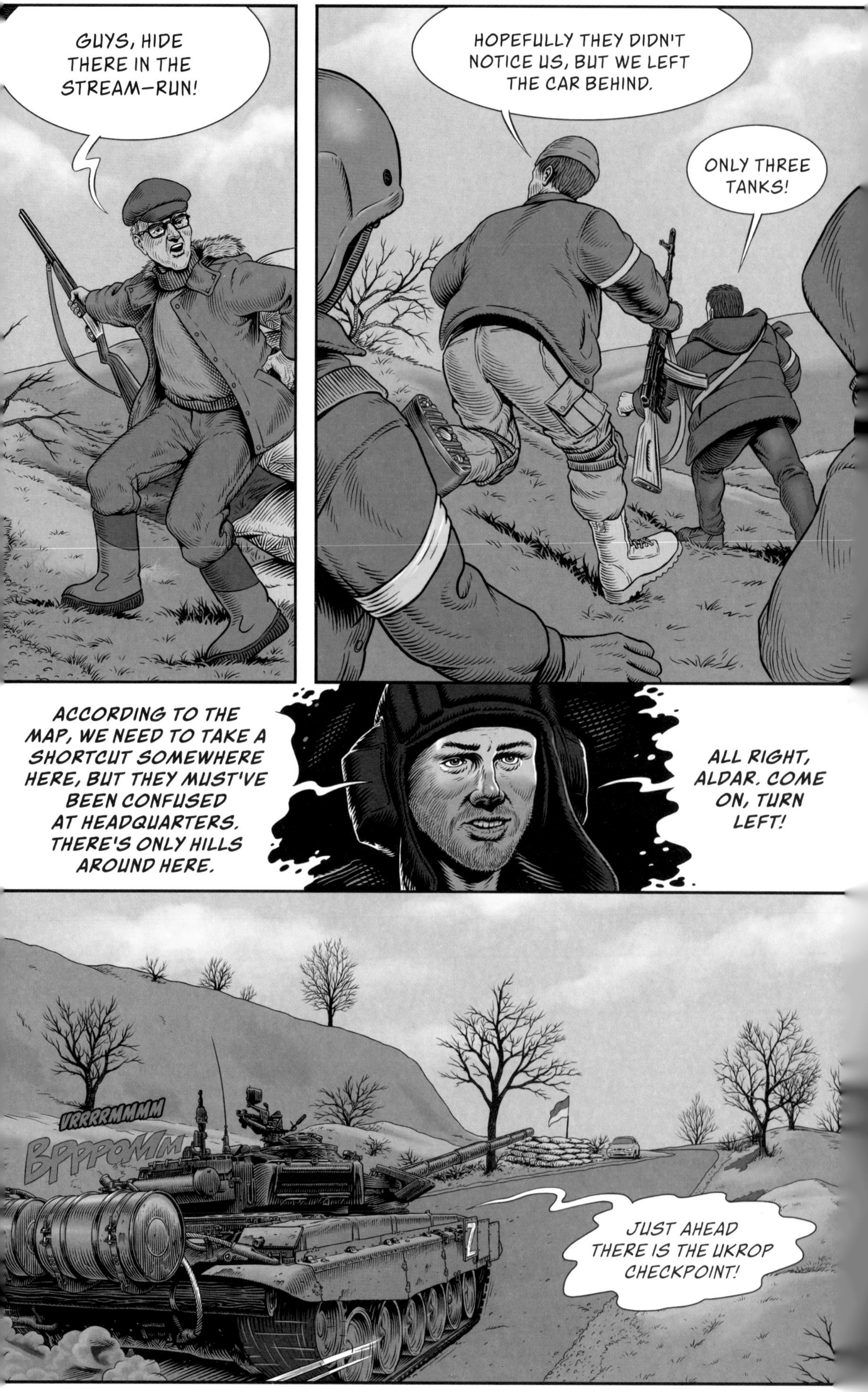
GUYS, HIDE THERE IN THE STREAM–RUN!
HOPEFULLY THEY DIDN'T NOTICE US, BUT WE LEFT THE CAR BEHIND.
ONLY THREE TANKS!
ACCORDING TO THE MAP, WE NEED TO TAKE A SHORTCUT SOMEWHERE HERE, BUT THEY MUST'VE BEEN CONFUSED AT HEADQUARTERS. THERE'S ONLY HILLS AROUND HERE.
ALL RIGHT, ALDAR. COME ON, TURN LEFT!
URRRRMMMM
BPPPOMM
JUST AHEAD THERE IS THE UKROP CHECKPOINT!

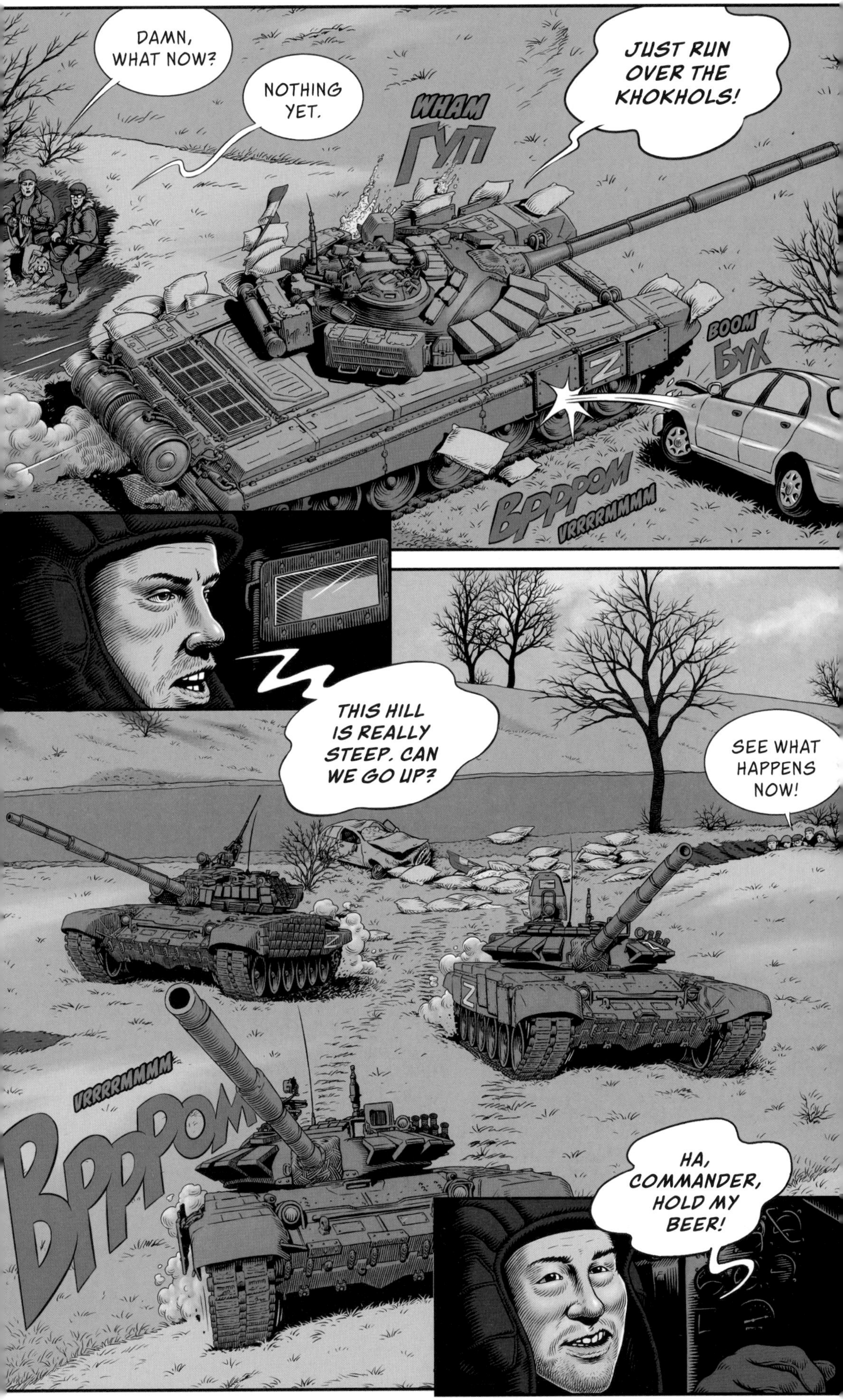
DAMN, WHAT NOW?
NOTHING YET.
JUST RUN OVER THE KHOKHOLS!
WHAM
ГУП
BOOM
БУХ
BPPPOM
VRRRRMMMM
THIS HILL IS REALLY STEEP. CAN WE GO UP?
SEE WHAT HAPPENS NOW!
VRRRRMMMM
BPPPOM
HA, COMMANDER, HOLD MY BEER!

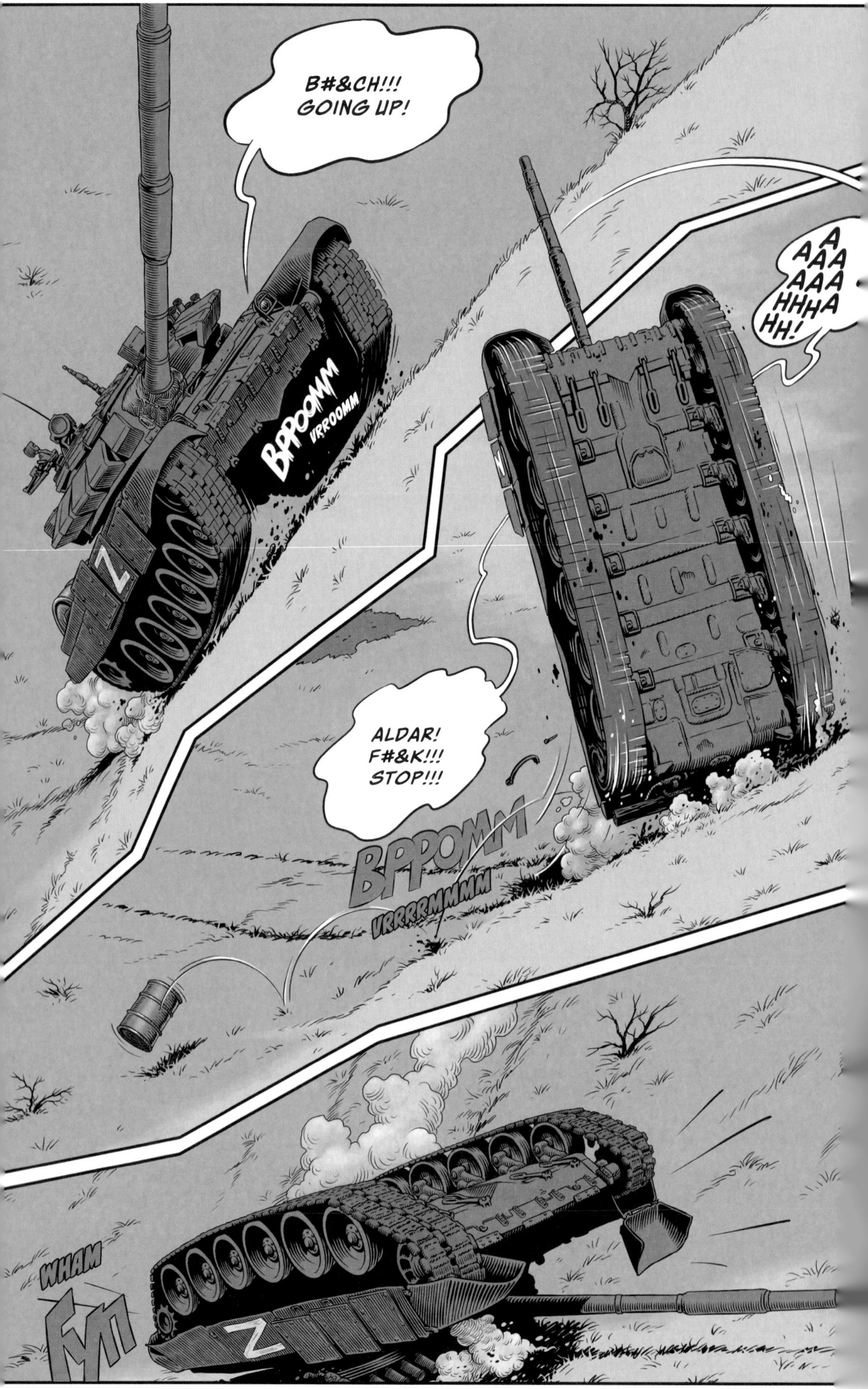
B#&CH!!! GOING UP!
BPPOOMM
VRROOMM
AAAAAAAHHHAHH!
ALDAR! F#&K!!! STOP!!!
BPPOMM
VRRRRMMMM
WHAM

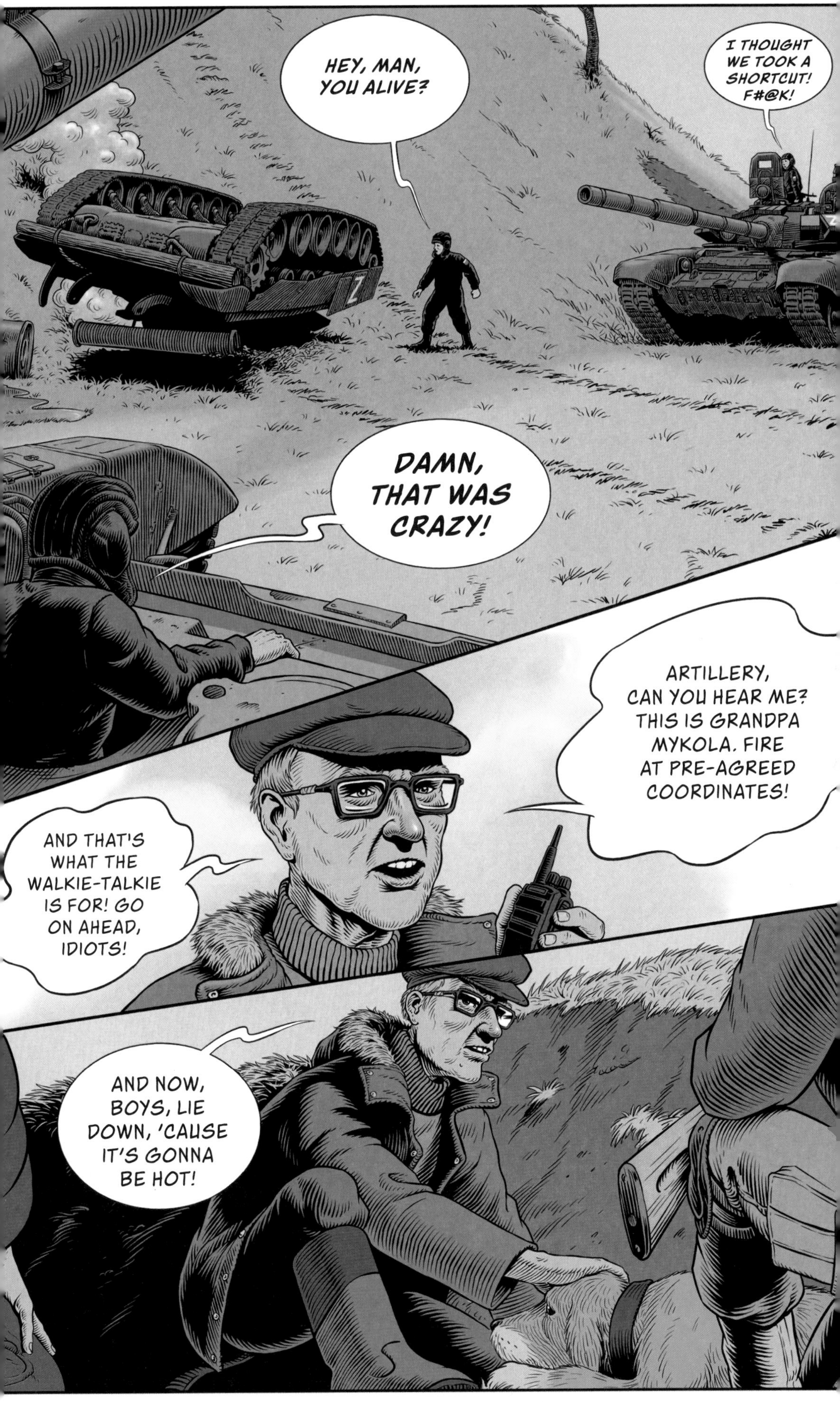
HEY, MAN, YOU ALIVE?
I THOUGHT WE TOOK A SHORTCUT! F#@K!
DAMN, THAT WAS CRAZY!
ARTILLERY, CAN YOU HEAR ME? THIS IS GRANDPA MYKOLA. FIRE AT PRE-AGREED COORDINATES!
AND THAT'S WHAT THE WALKIE-TALKIE IS FOR! GO ON AHEAD, IDIOTS!
AND NOW, BOYS, LIE DOWN, 'CAUSE IT'S GONNA BE HOT!

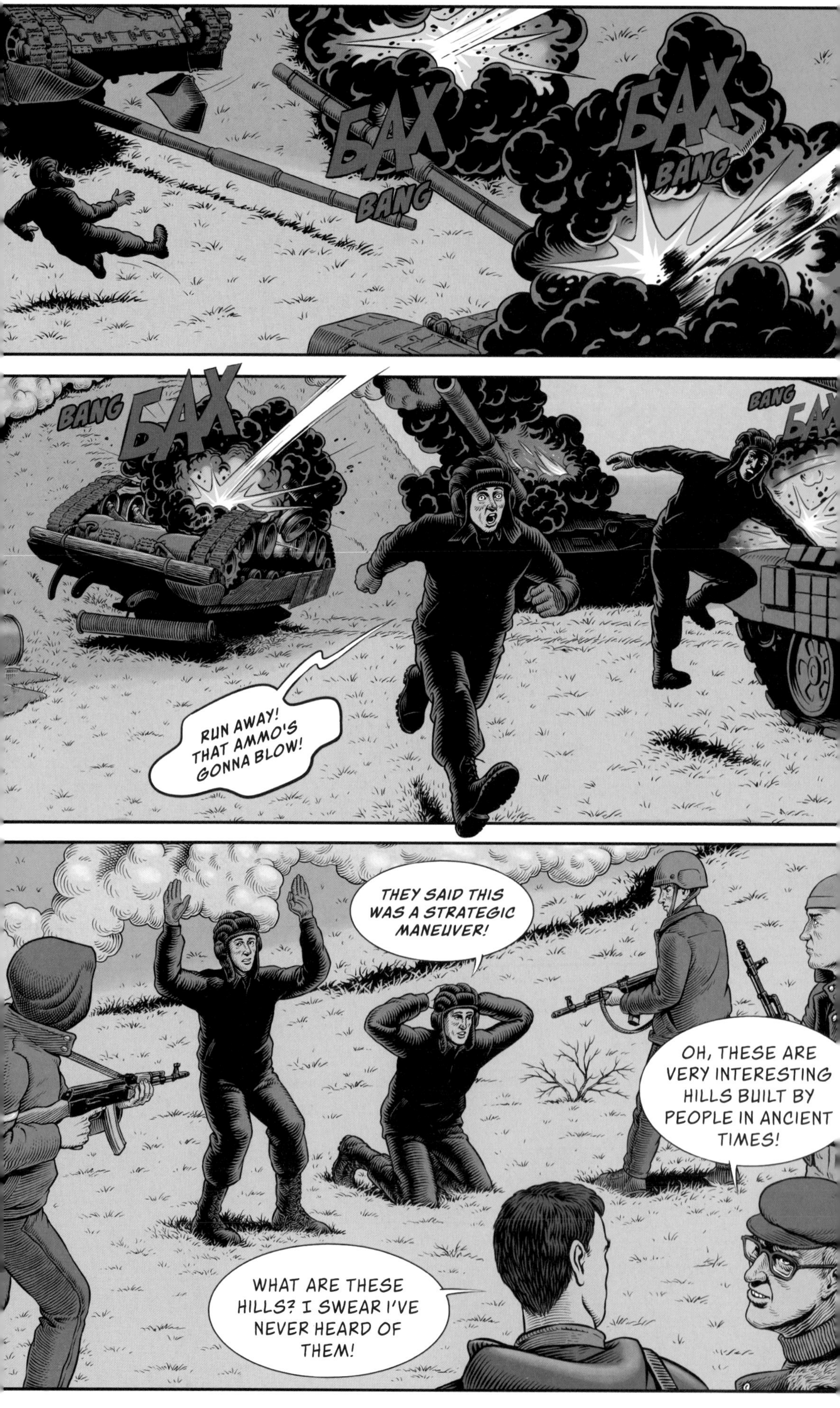
БАХ
BANG
БАХ
BANG
BANG
БАХ
BANG
RUN AWAY! THAT AMMO'S GONNA BLOW!
THEY SAID THIS WAS A STRATEGIC MANEUVER!
OH, THESE ARE VERY INTERESTING HILLS BUILT BY PEOPLE IN ANCIENT TIMES!
WHAT ARE THESE HILLS? I SWEAR I'VE NEVER HEARD OF THEM!

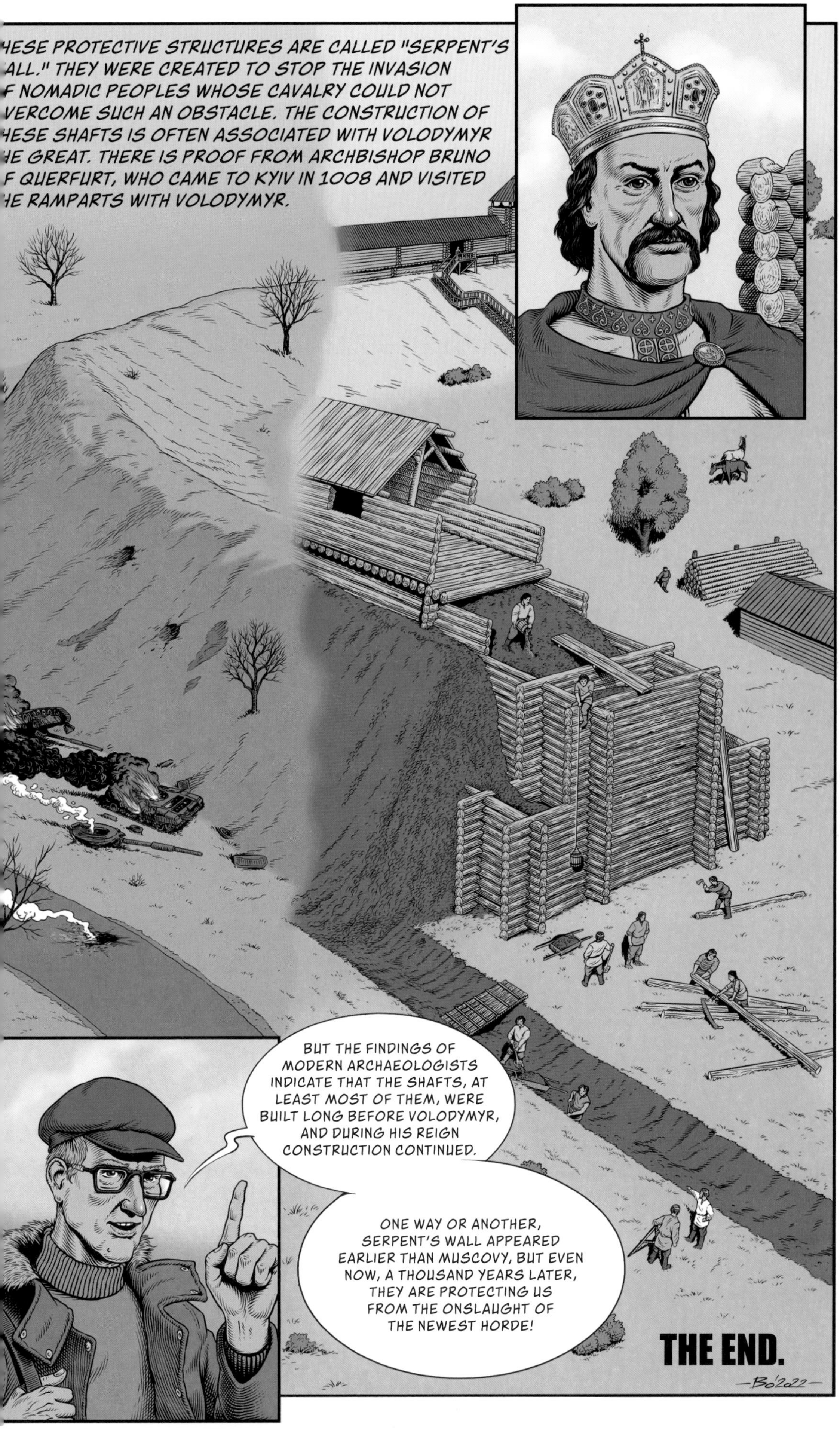

HESE PROTECTIVE STRUCTURES ARE CALLED "SERPENT'S ALL." THEY WERE CREATED TO STOP THE INVASION F NOMADIC PEOPLES WHOSE CAVALRY COULD NOT VERCOME SUCH AN OBSTACLE. THE CONSTRUCTION OF HESE SHAFTS IS OFTEN ASSOCIATED WITH VOLODYMYR HE GREAT. THERE IS PROOF FROM ARCHBISHOP BRUNO F QUERFURT, WHO CAME TO KYIV IN 1008 AND VISITED HE RAMPARTS WITH VOLODYMYR.
BUT THE FINDINGS OF MODERN ARCHAEOLOGISTS INDICATE THAT THE SHAFTS, AT LEAST MOST OF THEM, WERE BUILT LONG BEFORE VOLODYMYR, AND DURING HIS REIGN CONSTRUCTION CONTINUED.
ONE WAY OR ANOTHER, SERPENT'S WALL APPEARED EARLIER THAN MUSCOVY, BUT EVEN NOW, A THOUSAND YEARS LATER, THEY ARE PROTECTING US FROM THE ONSLAUGHT OF THE NEWEST HORDE!
THE END.
Bo'2022

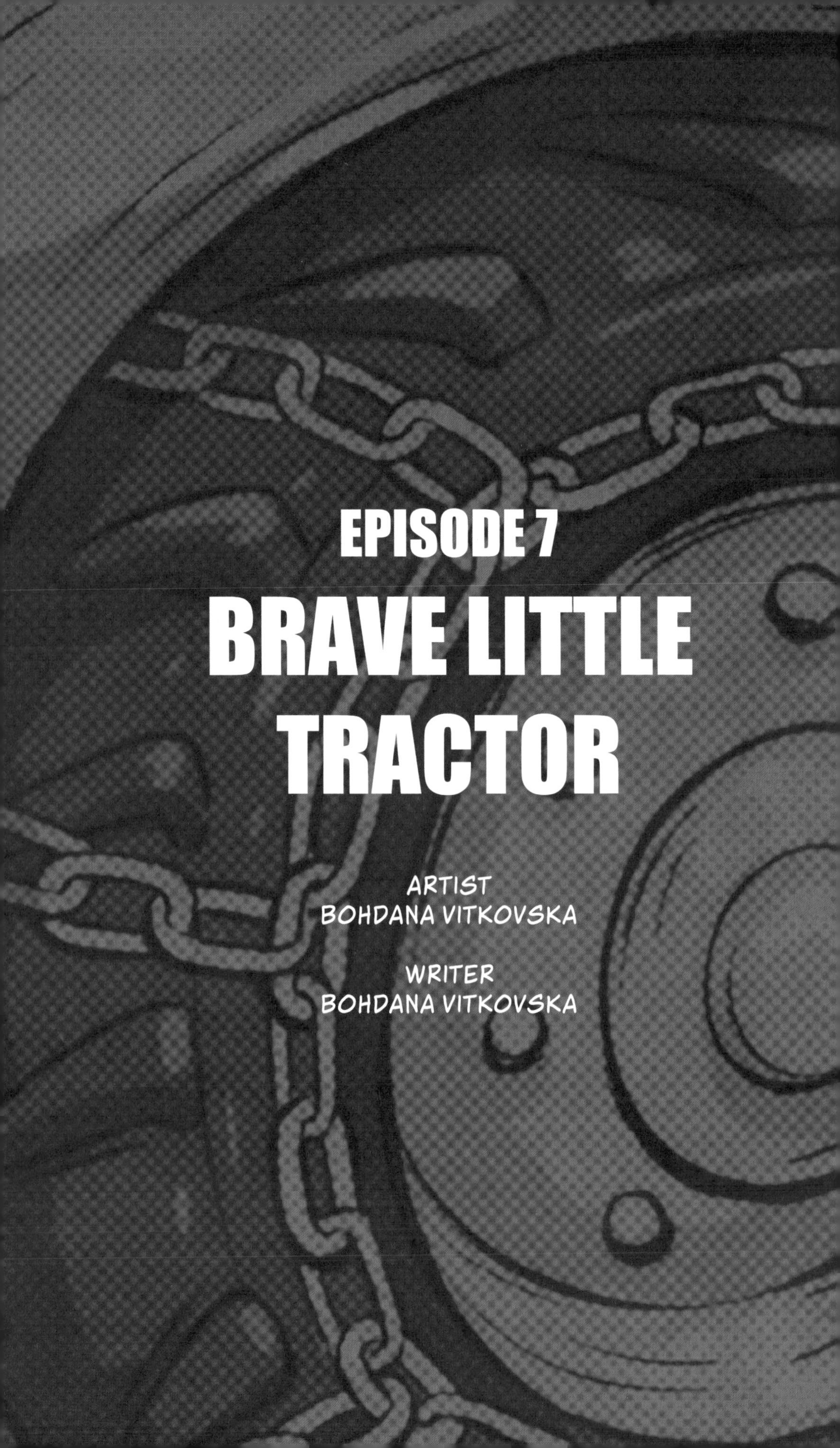

EPISODE 7
BRAVE LITTLE TRACTOR

ARTIST
BOHDANA VITKOVSKA

WRITER
BOHDANA VITKOVSKA

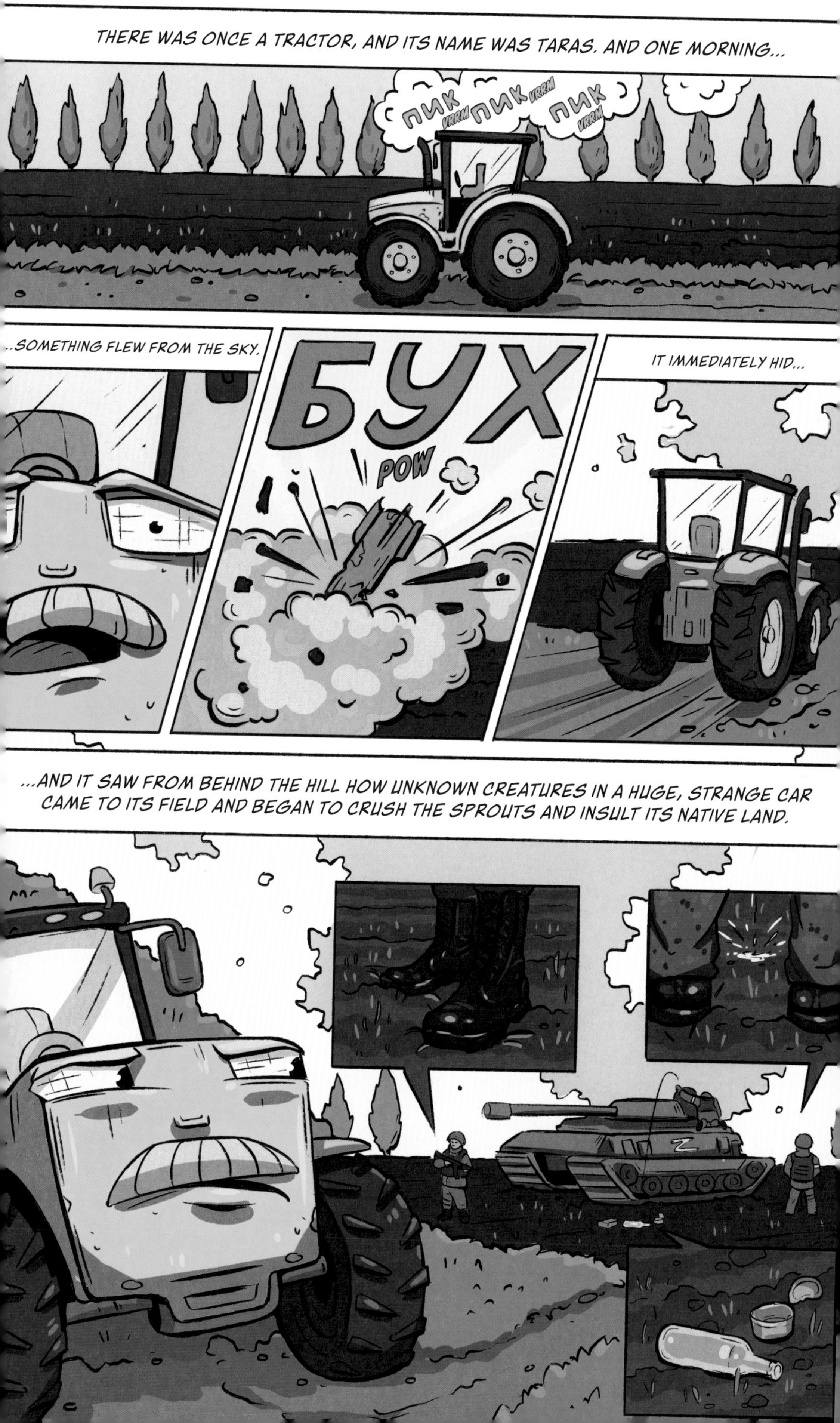
THERE WAS ONCE A TRACTOR, AND ITS NAME WAS TARAS. AND ONE MORNING...
ПИК VRRM ПИК VRRM ПИК VRRM
..SOMETHING FLEW FROM THE SKY.
БУХ
POW
IT IMMEDIATELY HID...
...AND IT SAW FROM BEHIND THE HILL HOW UNKNOWN CREATURES IN A HUGE, STRANGE CAR CAME TO ITS FIELD AND BEGAN TO CRUSH THE SPROUTS AND INSULT ITS NATIVE LAND.

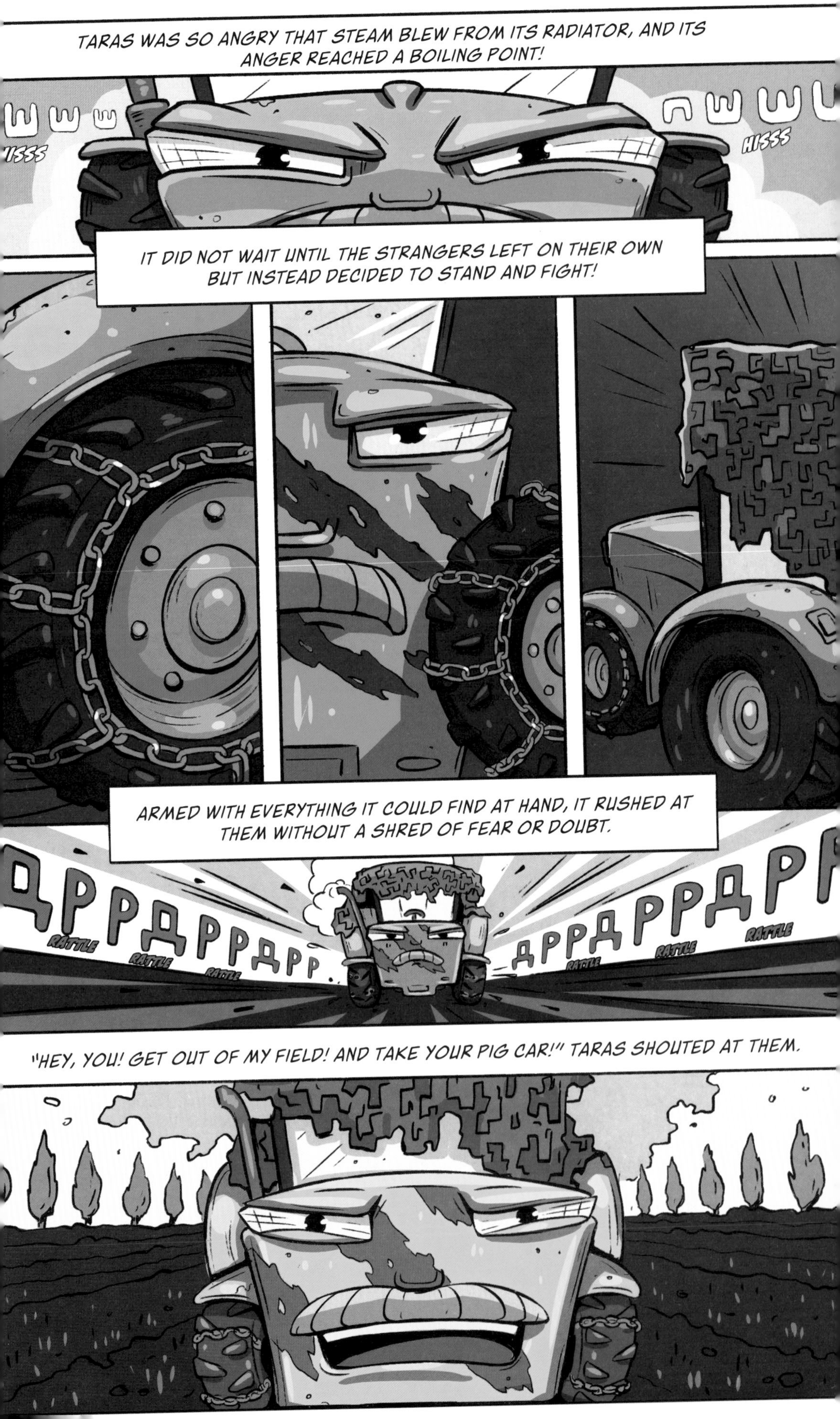
TARAS WAS SO ANGRY THAT STEAM BLEW FROM ITS RADIATOR, AND ITS ANGER REACHED A BOILING POINT!
ШШШ
ISSS
ПШШШ
HISSS
IT DID NOT WAIT UNTIL THE STRANGERS LEFT ON THEIR OWN BUT INSTEAD DECIDED TO STAND AND FIGHT!
ARMED WITH EVERYTHING IT COULD FIND AT HAND, IT RUSHED AT THEM WITHOUT A SHRED OF FEAR OR DOUBT.
ДРРДРРДРР
RATTLE
RATTLE
RATTLE
ДРРДРРДРР
RATTLE
RATTLE
RATTLE
"HEY, YOU! GET OUT OF MY FIELD! AND TAKE YOUR PIG CAR!" TARAS SHOUTED AT THEM.

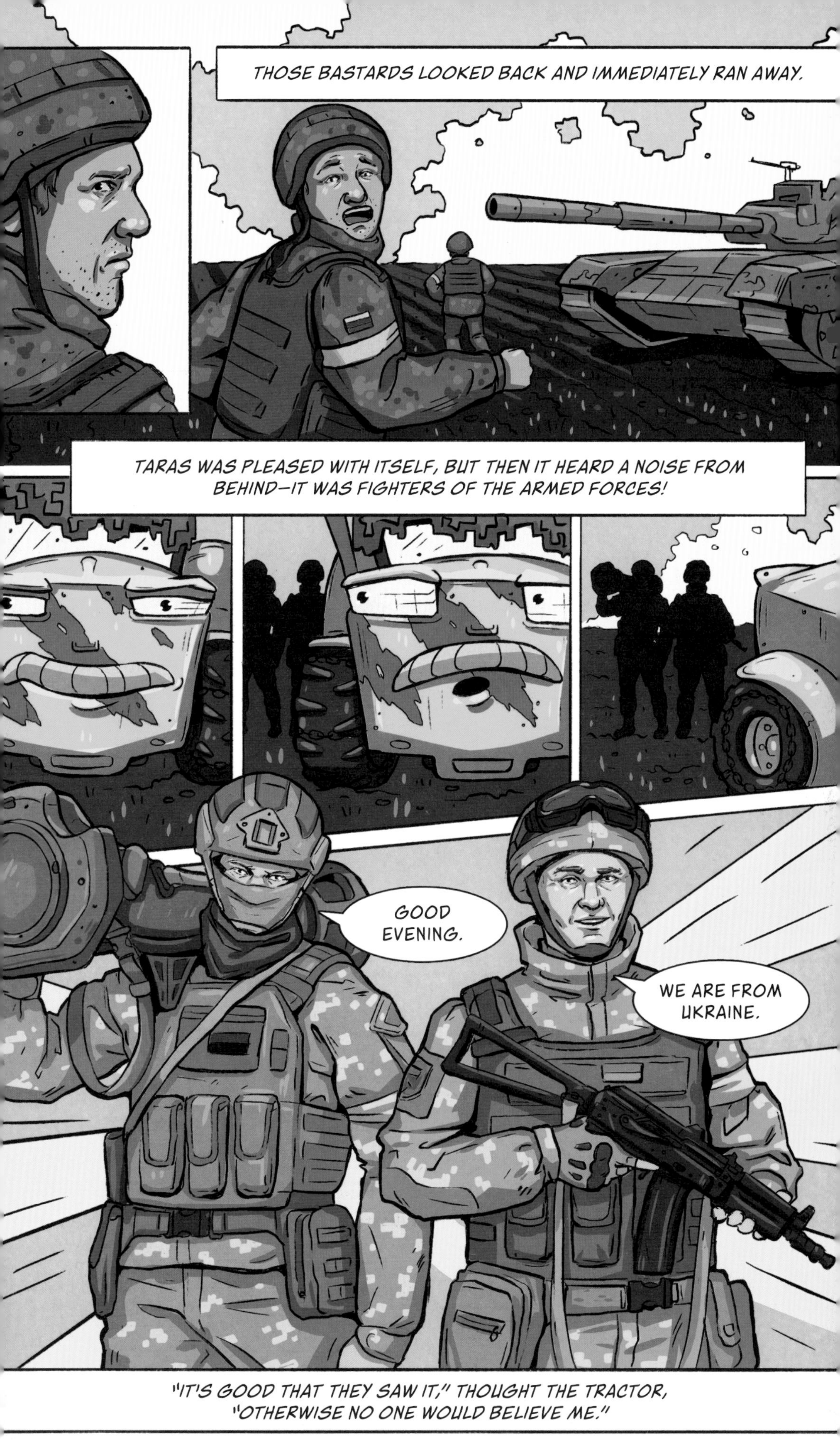
THOSE BASTARDS LOOKED BACK AND IMMEDIATELY RAN AWAY.
TARAS WAS PLEASED WITH ITSELF, BUT THEN IT HEARD A NOISE FROM BEHIND—IT WAS FIGHTERS OF THE ARMED FORCES!
GOOD EVENING.
WE ARE FROM UKRAINE.
"IT'S GOOD THAT THEY SAW IT," THOUGHT THE TRACTOR, "OTHERWISE NO ONE WOULD BELIEVE ME."

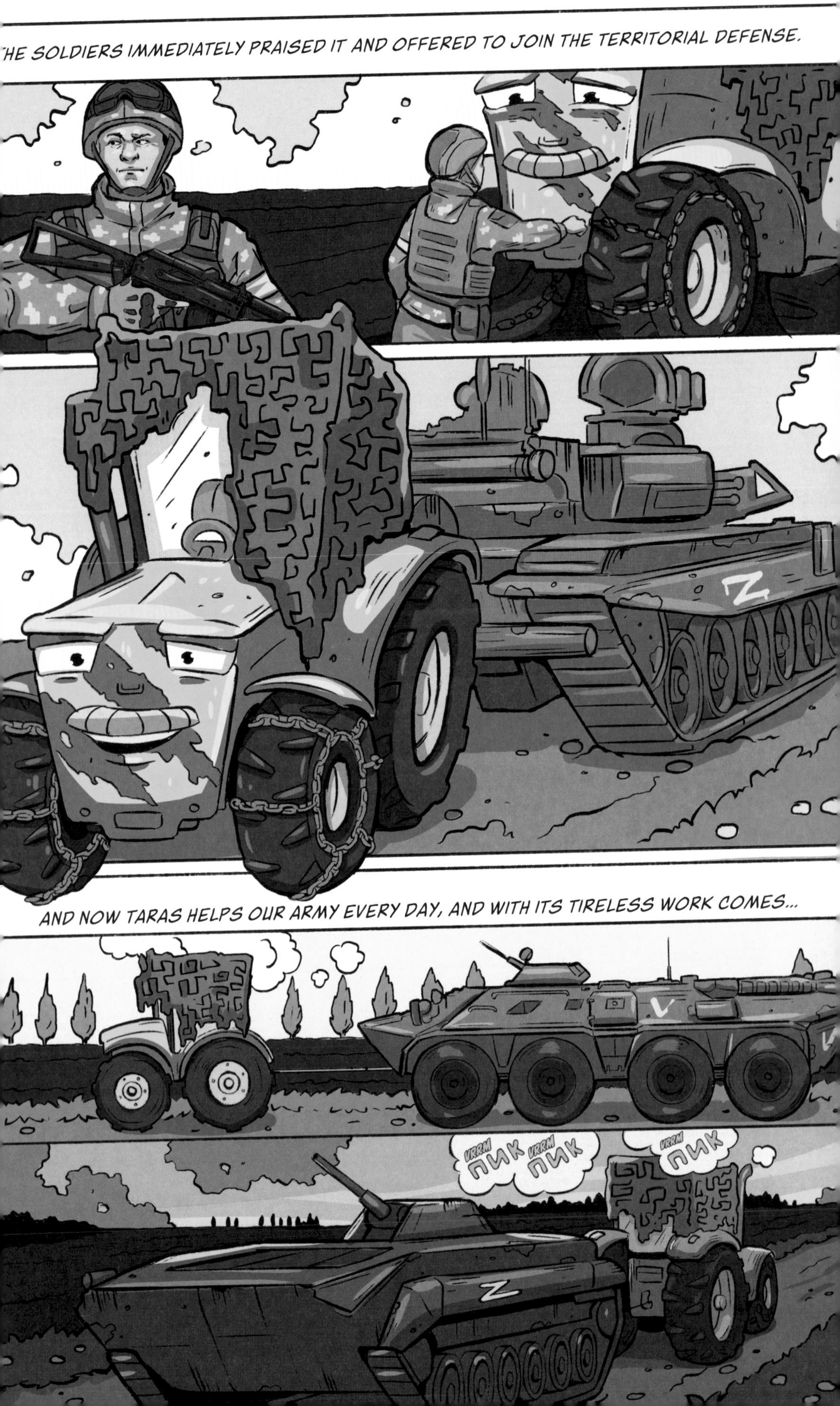
THE SOLDIERS IMMEDIATELY PRAISED IT AND OFFERED TO JOIN THE TERRITORIAL DEFENSE.
Z
AND NOW TARAS HELPS OUR ARMY EVERY DAY, AND WITH ITS TIRELESS WORK COMES...
V
VRRM ПИК
VRRM ПИК
VRRM ПИК
Z

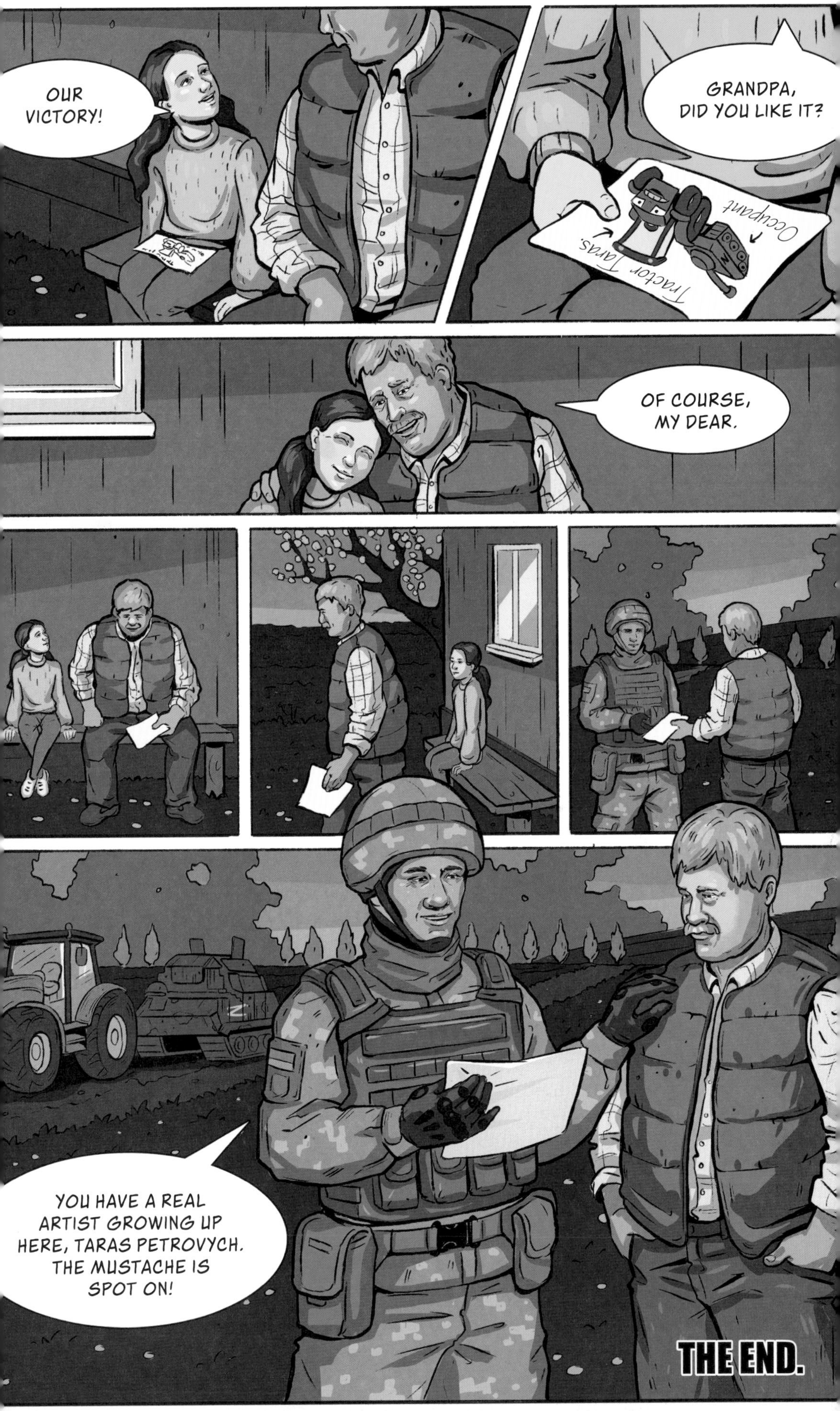
OUR VICTORY!
GRANDPA, DID YOU LIKE IT?
Tractor Taras.
Occupant
OF COURSE, MY DEAR.
YOU HAVE A REAL ARTIST GROWING UP HERE, TARAS PETROVYCH. THE MUSTACHE IS SPOT ON!
THE END.

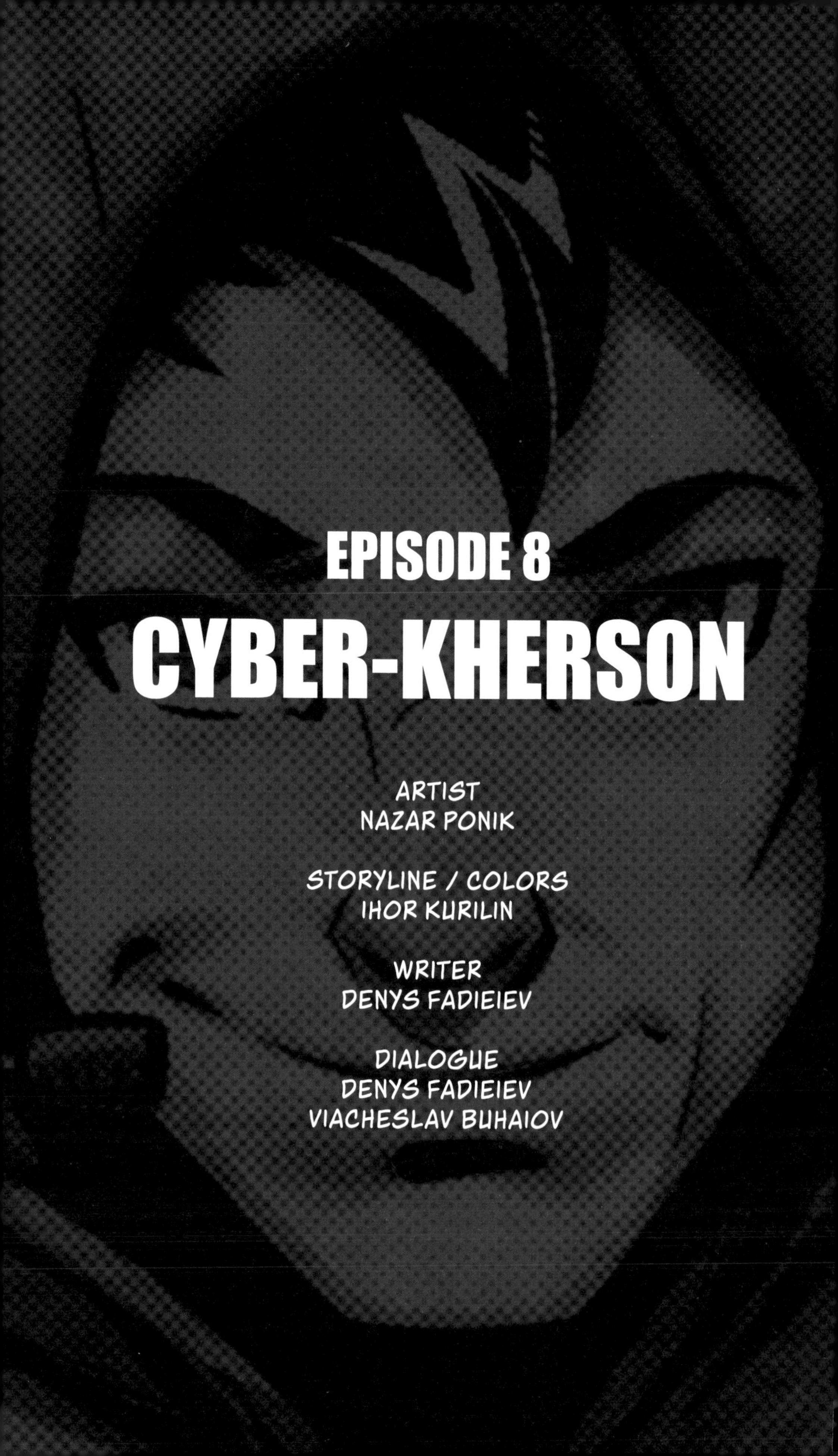

EPISODE 8
CYBER-KHERSON

ARTIST
NAZAR PONIK

STORYLINE / COLORS
IHOR KURILIN

WRITER
DENYS FADIEIEV

DIALOGUE
DENYS FADIEIEV
VIACHESLAV BUHAIOV

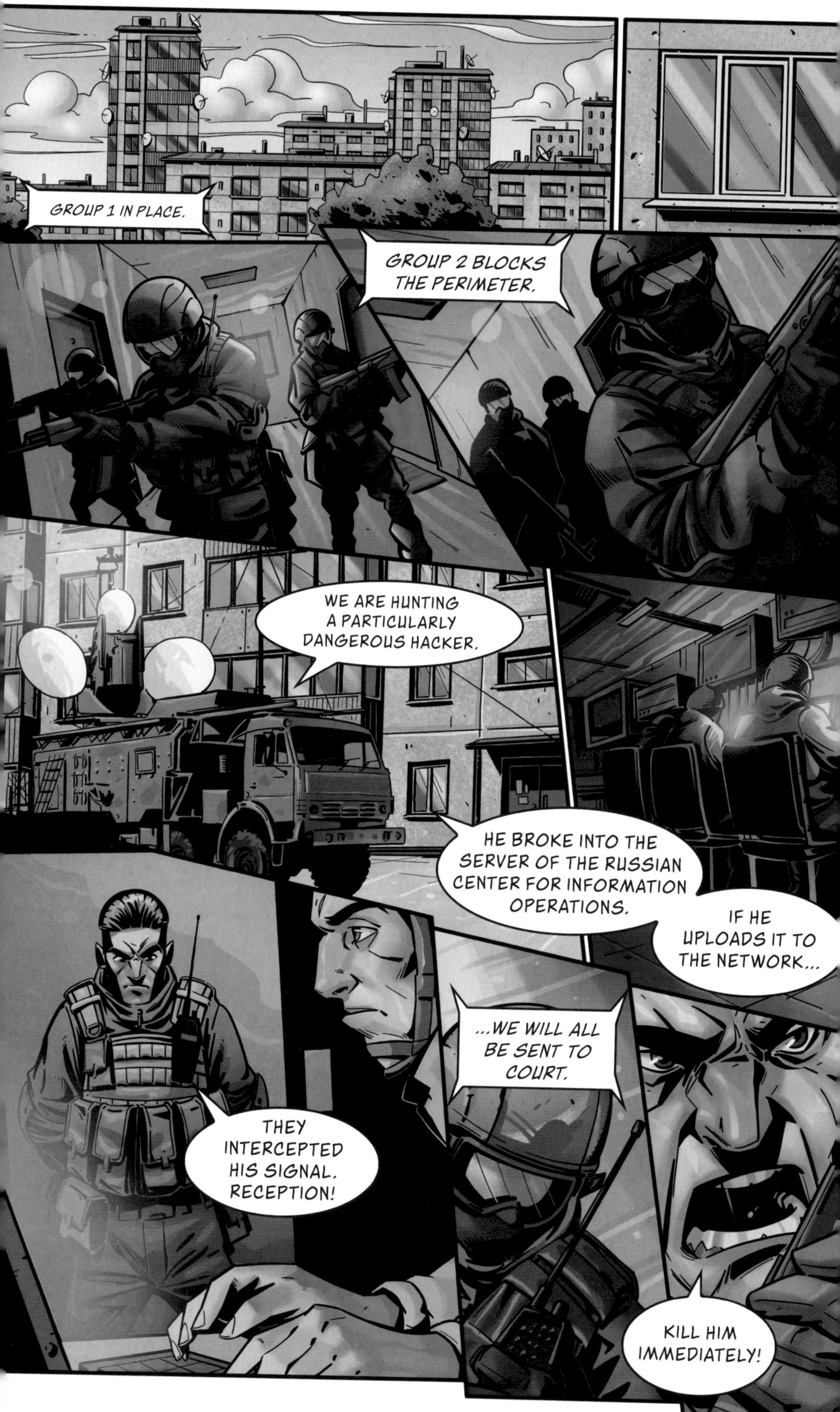
GROUP 1 IN PLACE.
GROUP 2 BLOCKS THE PERIMETER.
WE ARE HUNTING A PARTICULARLY DANGEROUS HACKER.
HE BROKE INTO THE SERVER OF THE RUSSIAN CENTER FOR INFORMATION OPERATIONS.
IF HE UPLOADS IT TO THE NETWORK...
...WE WILL ALL BE SENT TO COURT.
THEY INTERCEPTED HIS SIGNAL. RECEPTION!
KILL HIM IMMEDIATELY!

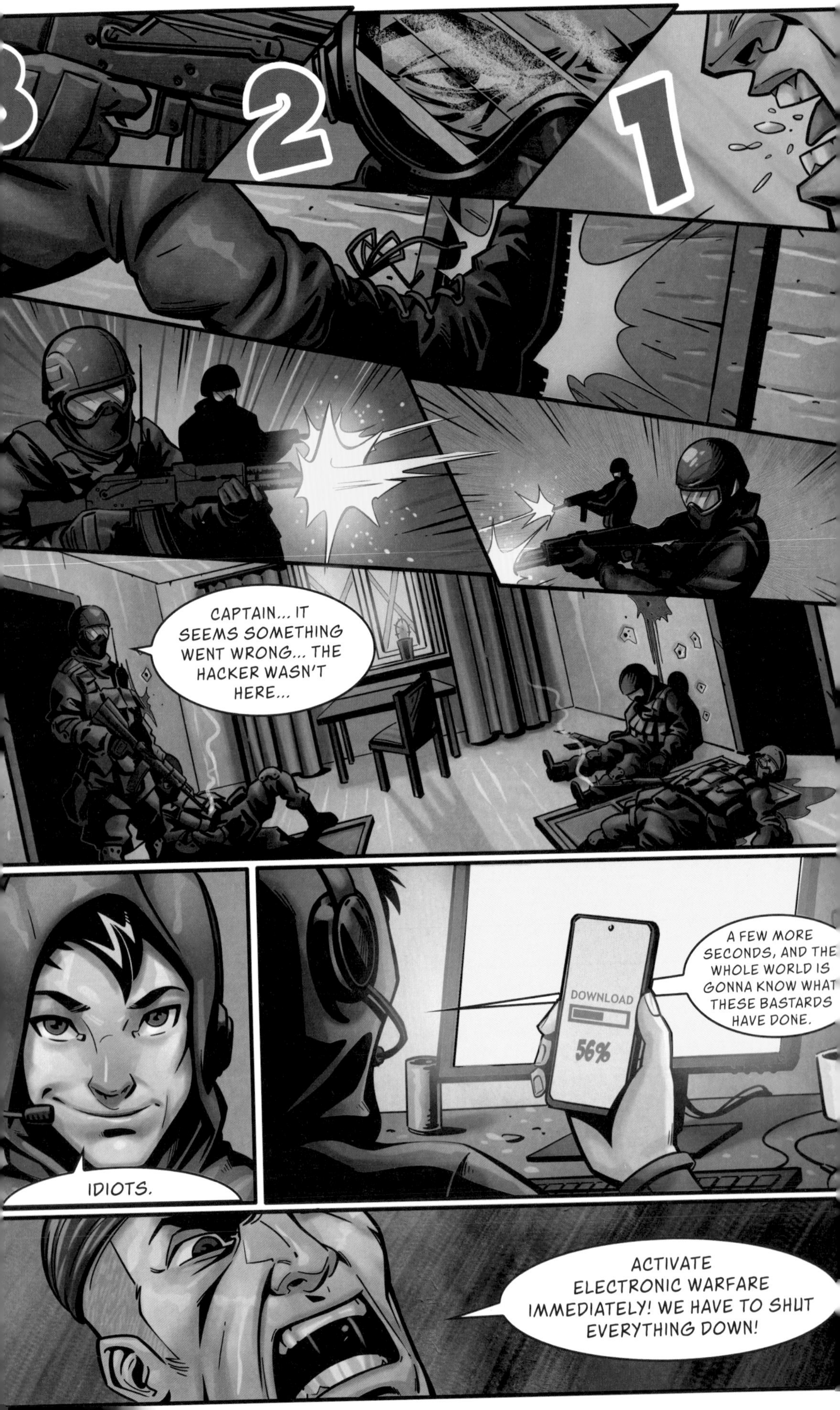
3
2
1
CAPTAIN... IT SEEMS SOMETHING WENT WRONG... THE HACKER WASN'T HERE...
IDIOTS.
DOWNLOAD
56%
A FEW MORE SECONDS, AND THE WHOLE WORLD IS GONNA KNOW WHAT THESE BASTARDS HAVE DONE.
ACTIVATE ELECTRONIC WARFARE IMMEDIATELY! WE HAVE TO SHUT EVERYTHING DOWN!

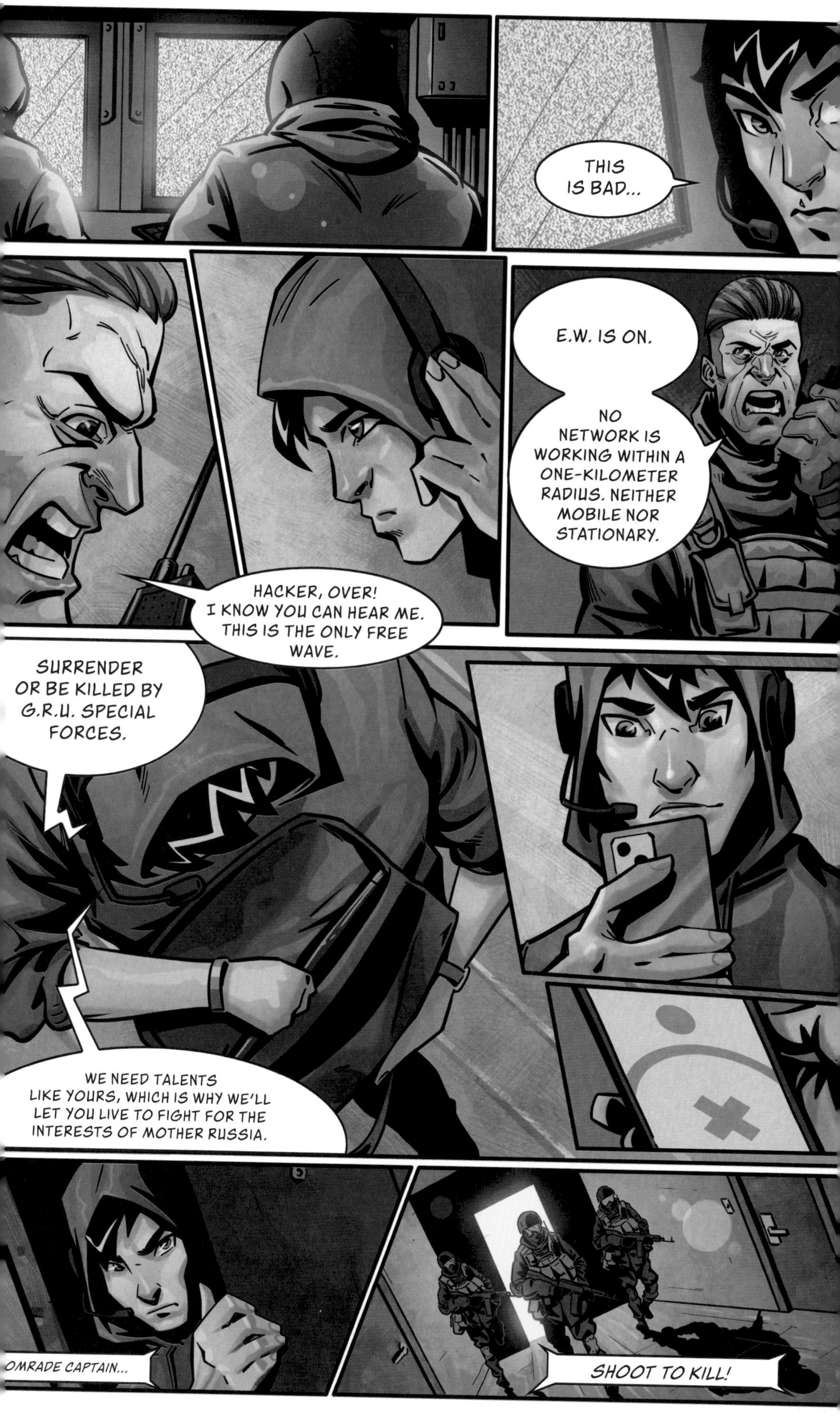
THIS IS BAD...
E.W. IS ON.
NO NETWORK IS WORKING WITHIN A ONE-KILOMETER RADIUS. NEITHER MOBILE NOR STATIONARY.
HACKER, OVER! I KNOW YOU CAN HEAR ME. THIS IS THE ONLY FREE WAVE.
SURRENDER OR BE KILLED BY G.R.U. SPECIAL FORCES.
WE NEED TALENTS LIKE YOURS, WHICH IS WHY WE'LL LET YOU LIVE TO FIGHT FOR THE INTERESTS OF MOTHER RUSSIA.
OMRADE CAPTAIN...
SHOOT TO KILL!

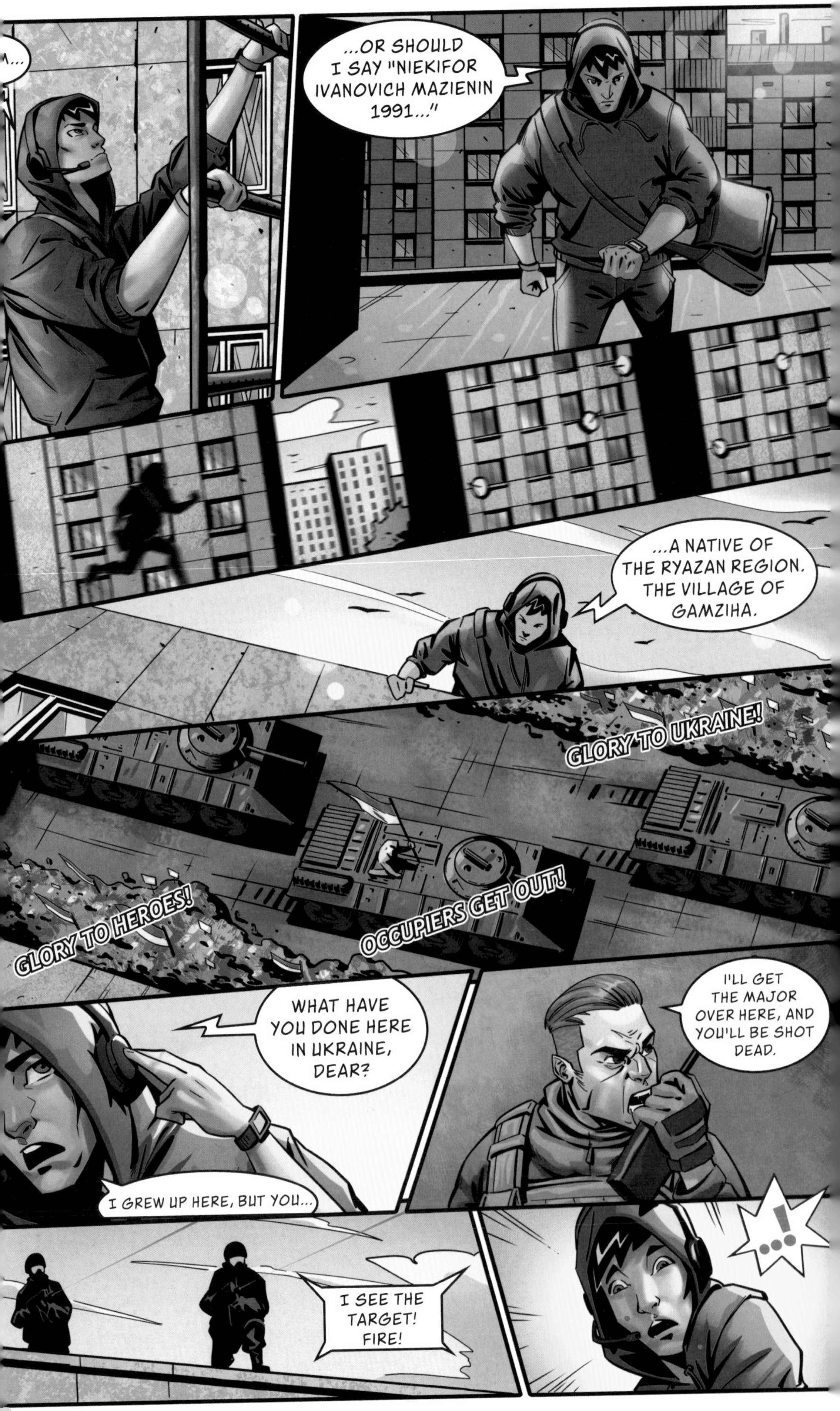
...OR SHOULD I SAY "NIEKIFOR IVANOVICH MAZIENIN 1991..."
...A NATIVE OF THE RYAZAN REGION. THE VILLAGE OF GAMZIHA.
GLORY TO UKRAINE!
OCCUPIERS GET OUT!
GLORY TO HEROES!
WHAT HAVE YOU DONE HERE IN UKRAINE, DEAR?
I GREW UP HERE, BUT YOU...
I'LL GET THE MAJOR OVER HERE, AND YOU'LL BE SHOT DEAD.
I SEE THE TARGET! FIRE!
!...

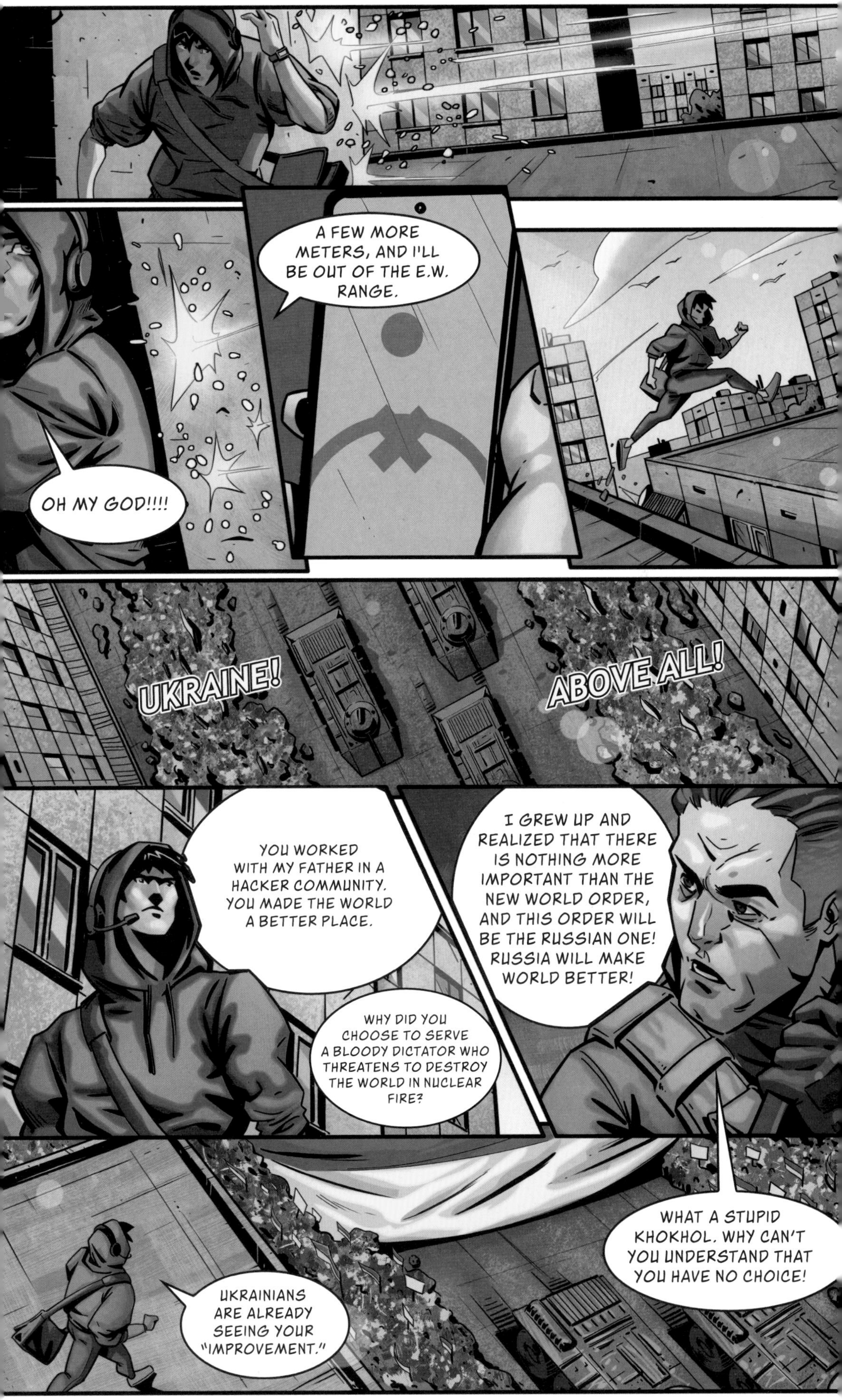
A FEW MORE METERS, AND I'LL BE OUT OF THE E.W. RANGE.
OH MY GOD!!!!
UKRAINE!
ABOVE ALL!
YOU WORKED WITH MY FATHER IN A HACKER COMMUNITY. YOU MADE THE WORLD A BETTER PLACE.
I GREW UP AND REALIZED THAT THERE IS NOTHING MORE IMPORTANT THAN THE NEW WORLD ORDER, AND THIS ORDER WILL BE THE RUSSIAN ONE! RUSSIA WILL MAKE WORLD BETTER!
WHY DID YOU CHOOSE TO SERVE A BLOODY DICTATOR WHO THREATENS TO DESTROY THE WORLD IN NUCLEAR FIRE?
WHAT A STUPID KHOKHOL. WHY CAN'T YOU UNDERSTAND THAT YOU HAVE NO CHOICE!
UKRAINIANS ARE ALREADY SEEING YOUR "IMPROVEMENT."

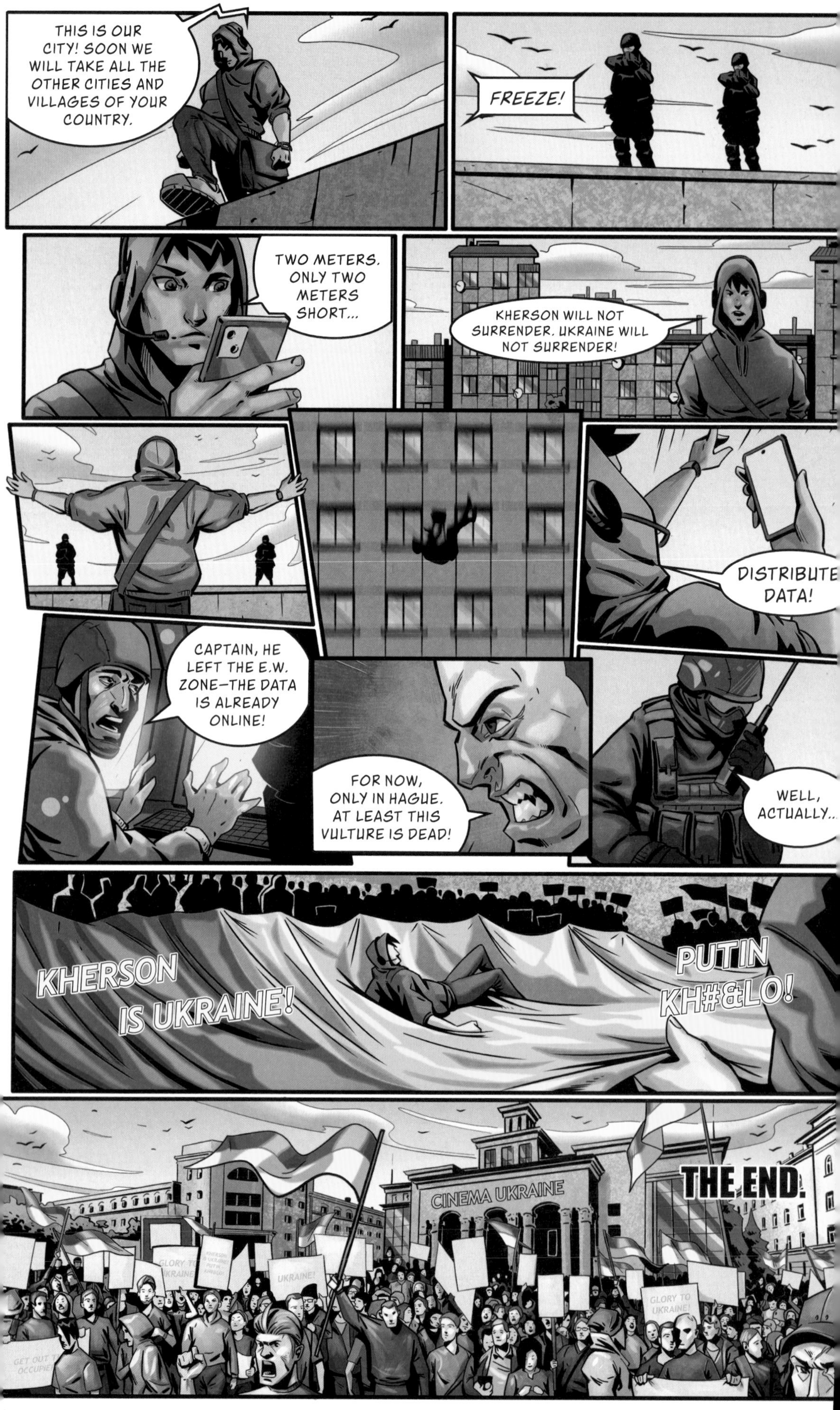
THIS IS OUR CITY! SOON WE WILL TAKE ALL THE OTHER CITIES AND VILLAGES OF YOUR COUNTRY.
FREEZE!
TWO METERS. ONLY TWO METERS SHORT...
KHERSON WILL NOT SURRENDER. UKRAINE WILL NOT SURRENDER!
DISTRIBUTE DATA!
CAPTAIN, HE LEFT THE E.W. ZONE—THE DATA IS ALREADY ONLINE!
FOR NOW, ONLY IN HAGUE. AT LEAST THIS VULTURE IS DEAD!
WELL, ACTUALLY...
KHERSON IS UKRAINE!
PUTIN KH#&LO!
CINEMA UKRAINE
THE END.
GLORY TO UKRAINE!
UKRAINE!
GLORY TO UKRAINE!

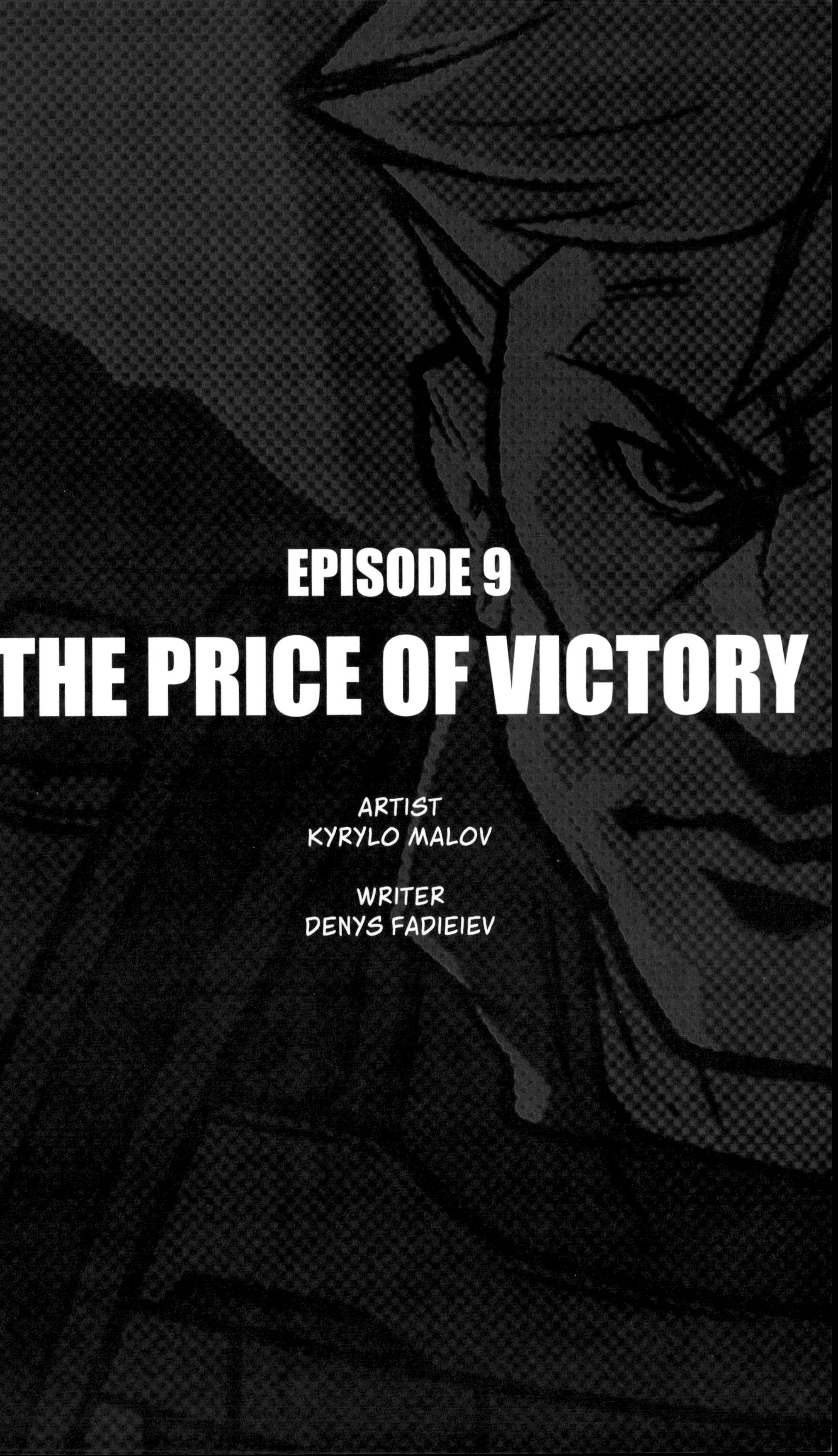

EPISODE 9
THE PRICE OF VICTORY

ARTIST
KYRYLO MALOV

WRITER
DENYS FADIEIEV

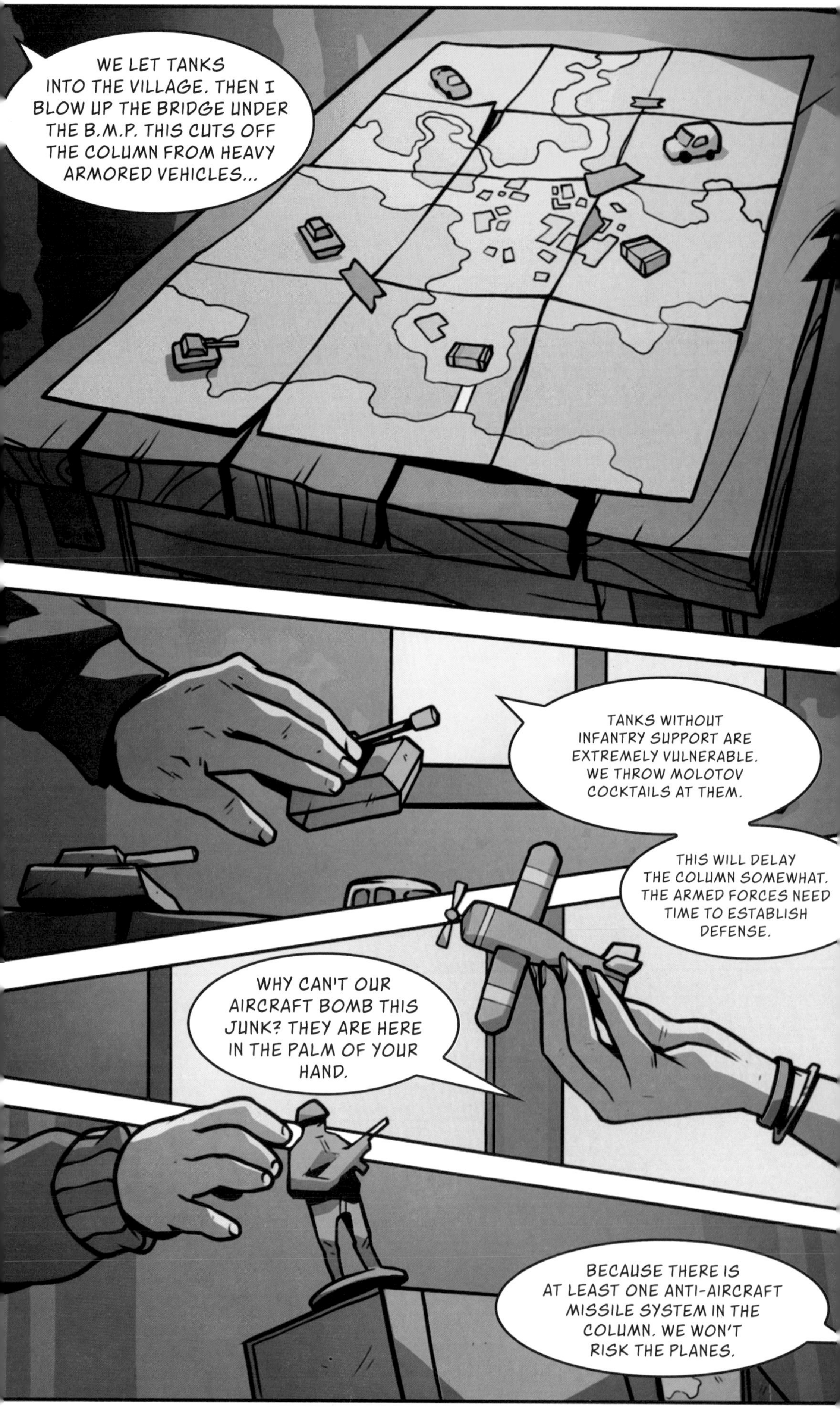

WE LET TANKS INTO THE VILLAGE. THEN I BLOW UP THE BRIDGE UNDER THE B.M.P. THIS CUTS OFF THE COLUMN FROM HEAVY ARMORED VEHICLES...
TANKS WITHOUT INFANTRY SUPPORT ARE EXTREMELY VULNERABLE. WE THROW MOLOTOV COCKTAILS AT THEM.
THIS WILL DELAY THE COLUMN SOMEWHAT. THE ARMED FORCES NEED TIME TO ESTABLISH DEFENSE.
WHY CAN'T OUR AIRCRAFT BOMB THIS JUNK? THEY ARE HERE IN THE PALM OF YOUR HAND.
BECAUSE THERE IS AT LEAST ONE ANTI-AIRCRAFT MISSILE SYSTEM IN THE COLUMN. WE WON'T RISK THE PLANES.

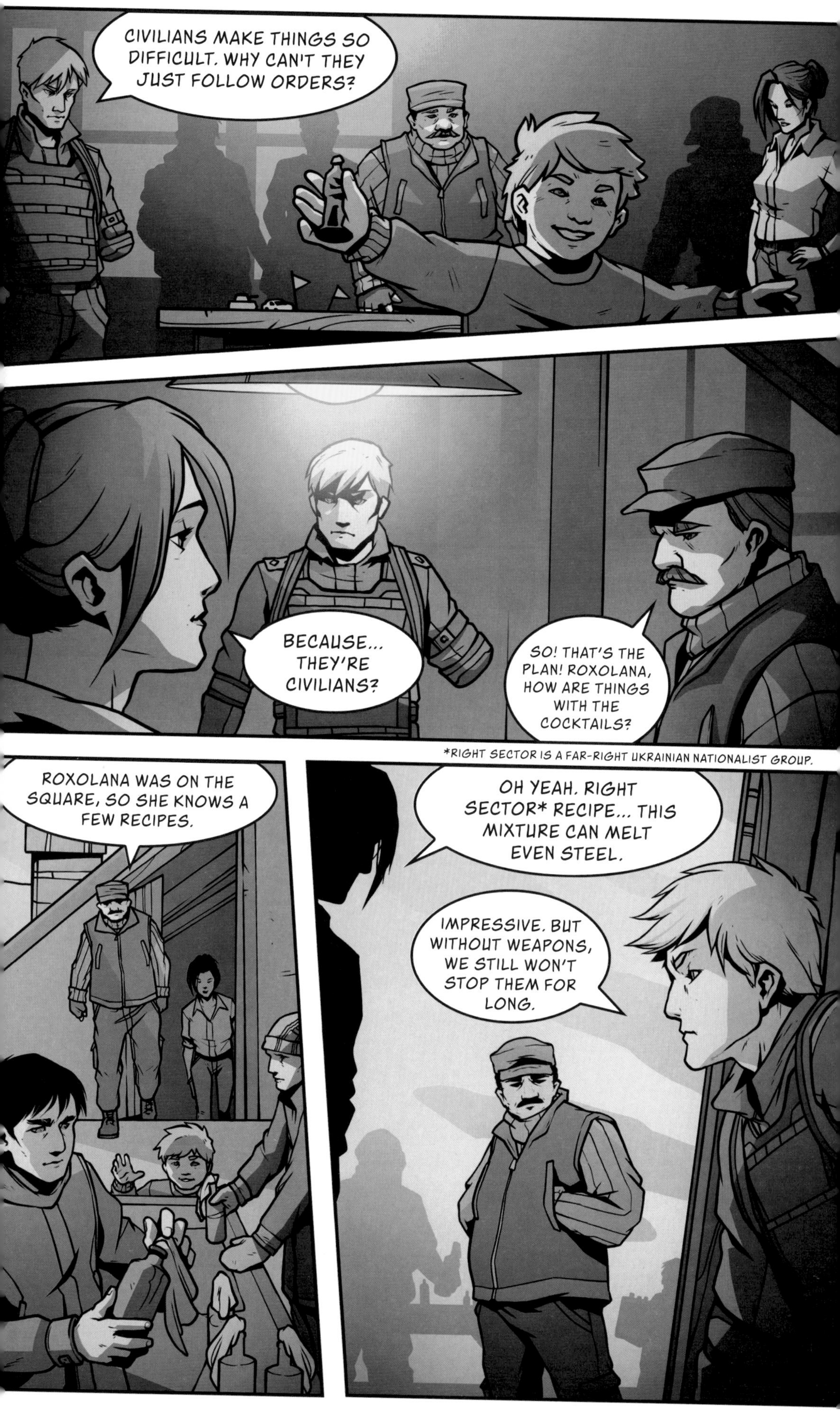
CIVILIANS MAKE THINGS SO DIFFICULT. WHY CAN'T THEY JUST FOLLOW ORDERS?
BECAUSE... THEY'RE CIVILIANS?
SO! THAT'S THE PLAN! ROXOLANA, HOW ARE THINGS WITH THE COCKTAILS?
ROXOLANA WAS ON THE SQUARE, SO SHE KNOWS A FEW RECIPES.
OH YEAH. RIGHT SECTOR* RECIPE... THIS MIXTURE CAN MELT EVEN STEEL.
IMPRESSIVE. BUT WITHOUT WEAPONS, WE STILL WON'T STOP THEM FOR LONG.

*RIGHT SECTOR IS A FAR-RIGHT UKRAINIAN NATIONALIST GROUP.

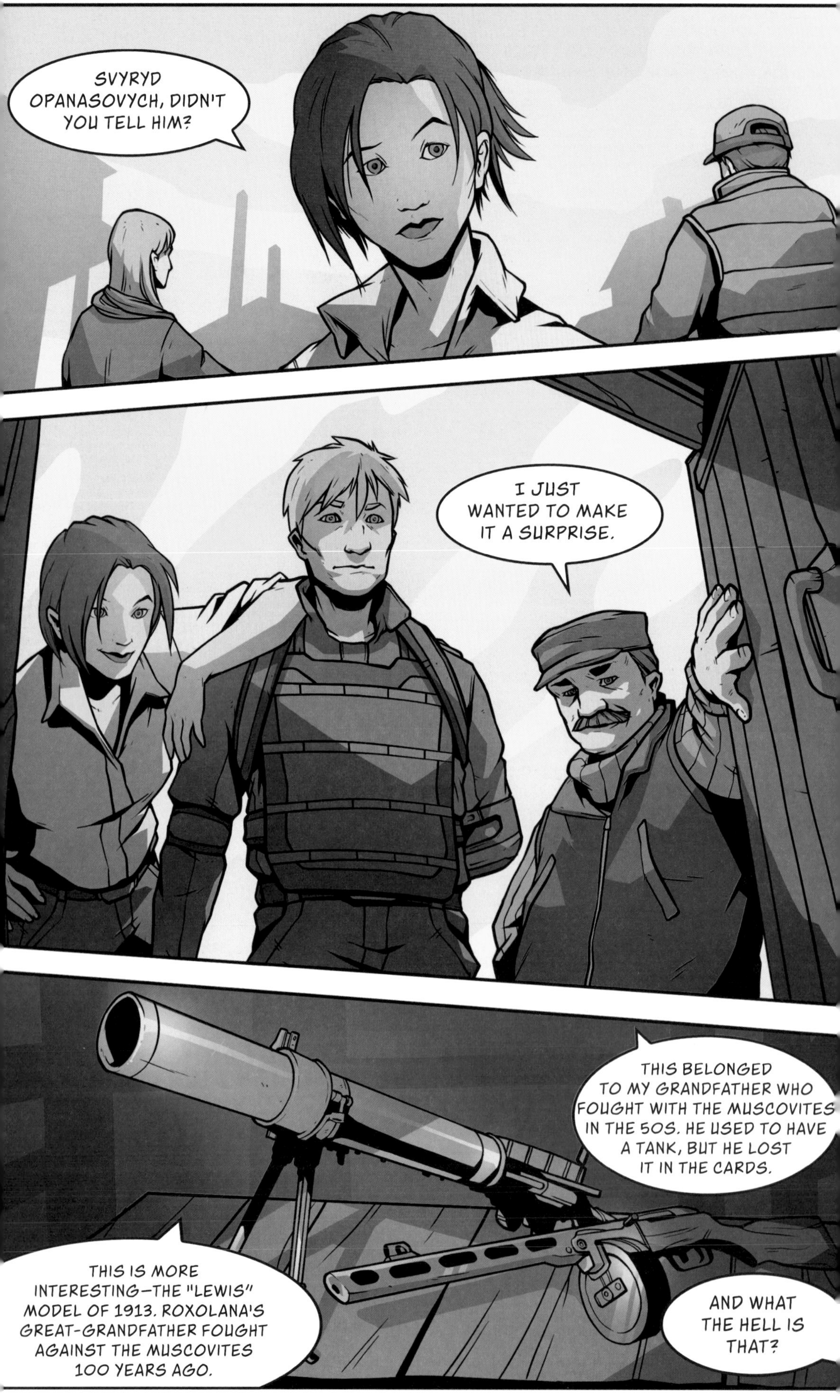
SVYRYD OPANASOVYCH, DIDN'T YOU TELL HIM?
I JUST WANTED TO MAKE IT A SURPRISE.
THIS BELONGED TO MY GRANDFATHER WHO FOUGHT WITH THE MUSCOVITES IN THE 50S. HE USED TO HAVE A TANK, BUT HE LOST IT IN THE CARDS.
THIS IS MORE INTERESTING—THE "LEWIS" MODEL OF 1913. ROXOLANA'S GREAT-GRANDFATHER FOUGHT AGAINST THE MUSCOVITES 100 YEARS AGO.
AND WHAT THE HELL IS THAT?

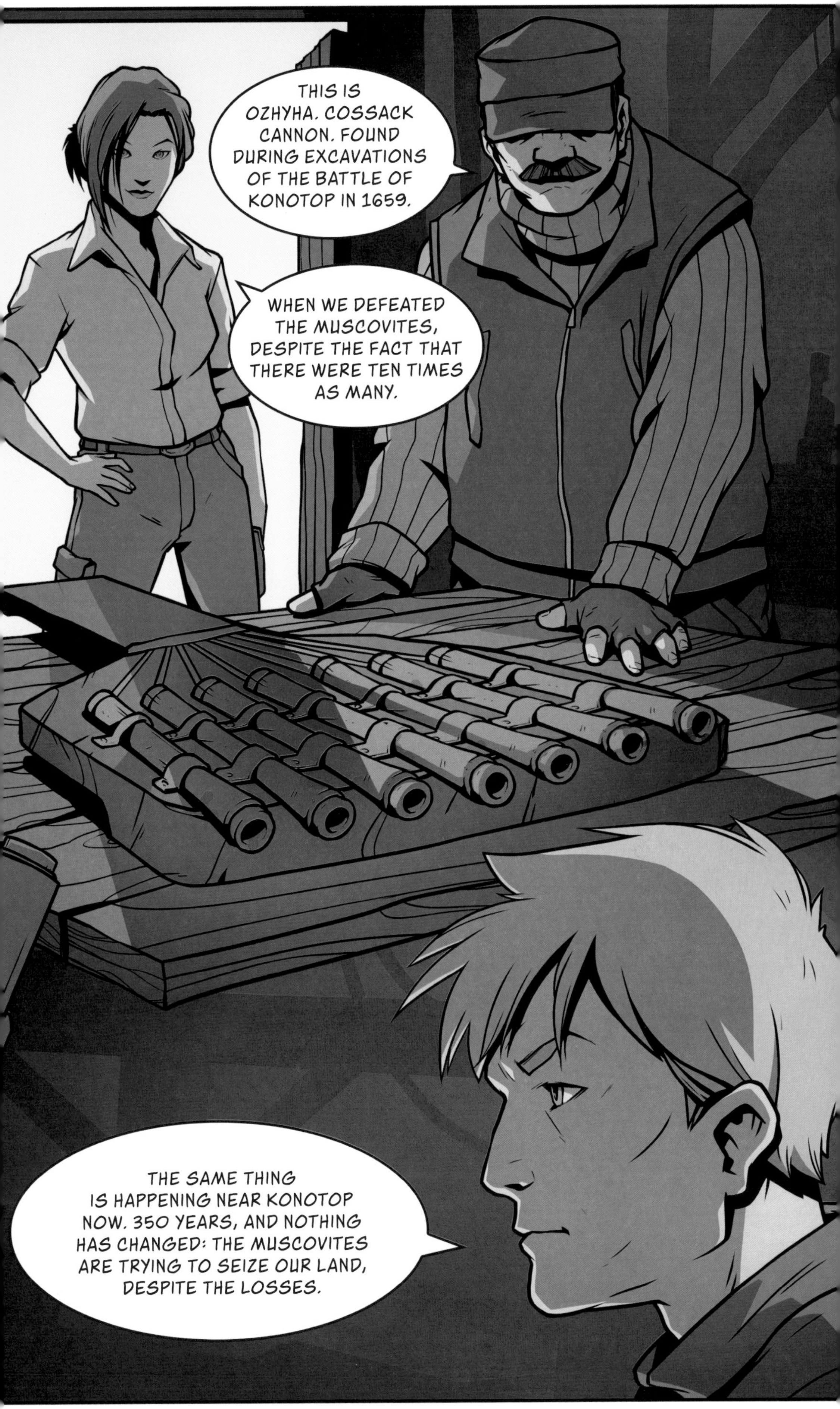
THIS IS OZHYHA. COSSACK CANNON. FOUND DURING EXCAVATIONS OF THE BATTLE OF KONOTOP IN 1659.
WHEN WE DEFEATED THE MUSCOVITES, DESPITE THE FACT THAT THERE WERE TEN TIMES AS MANY.
THE SAME THING IS HAPPENING NEAR KONOTOP NOW. 350 YEARS, AND NOTHING HAS CHANGED: THE MUSCOVITES ARE TRYING TO SEIZE OUR LAND, DESPITE THE LOSSES.

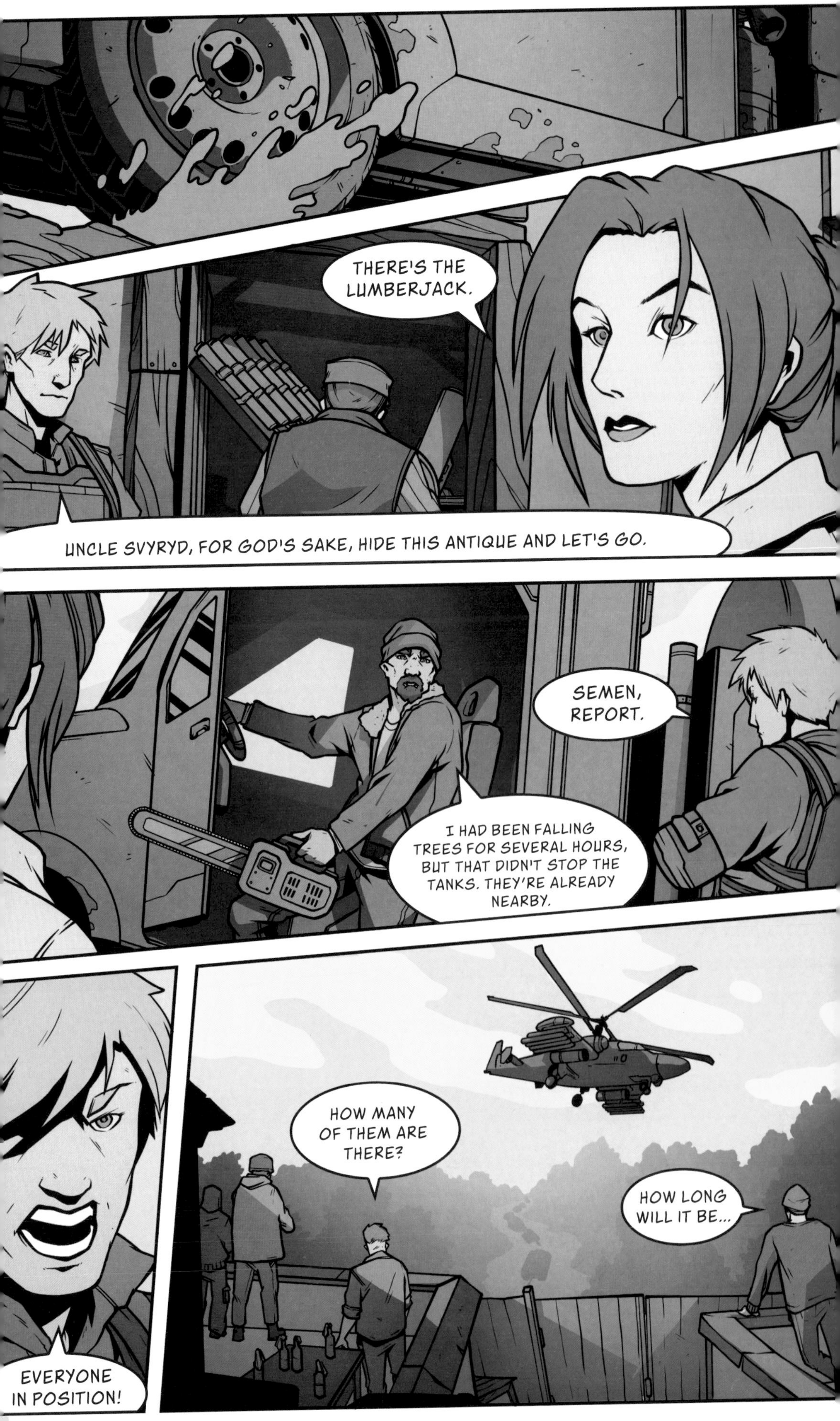
THERE'S THE LUMBERJACK.
UNCLE SVYRYD, FOR GOD'S SAKE, HIDE THIS ANTIQUE AND LET'S GO.
SEMEN, REPORT.
I HAD BEEN FALLING TREES FOR SEVERAL HOURS, BUT THAT DIDN'T STOP THE TANKS. THEY'RE ALREADY NEARBY.
EVERYONE IN POSITION!
HOW MANY OF THEM ARE THERE?
HOW LONG WILL IT BE...

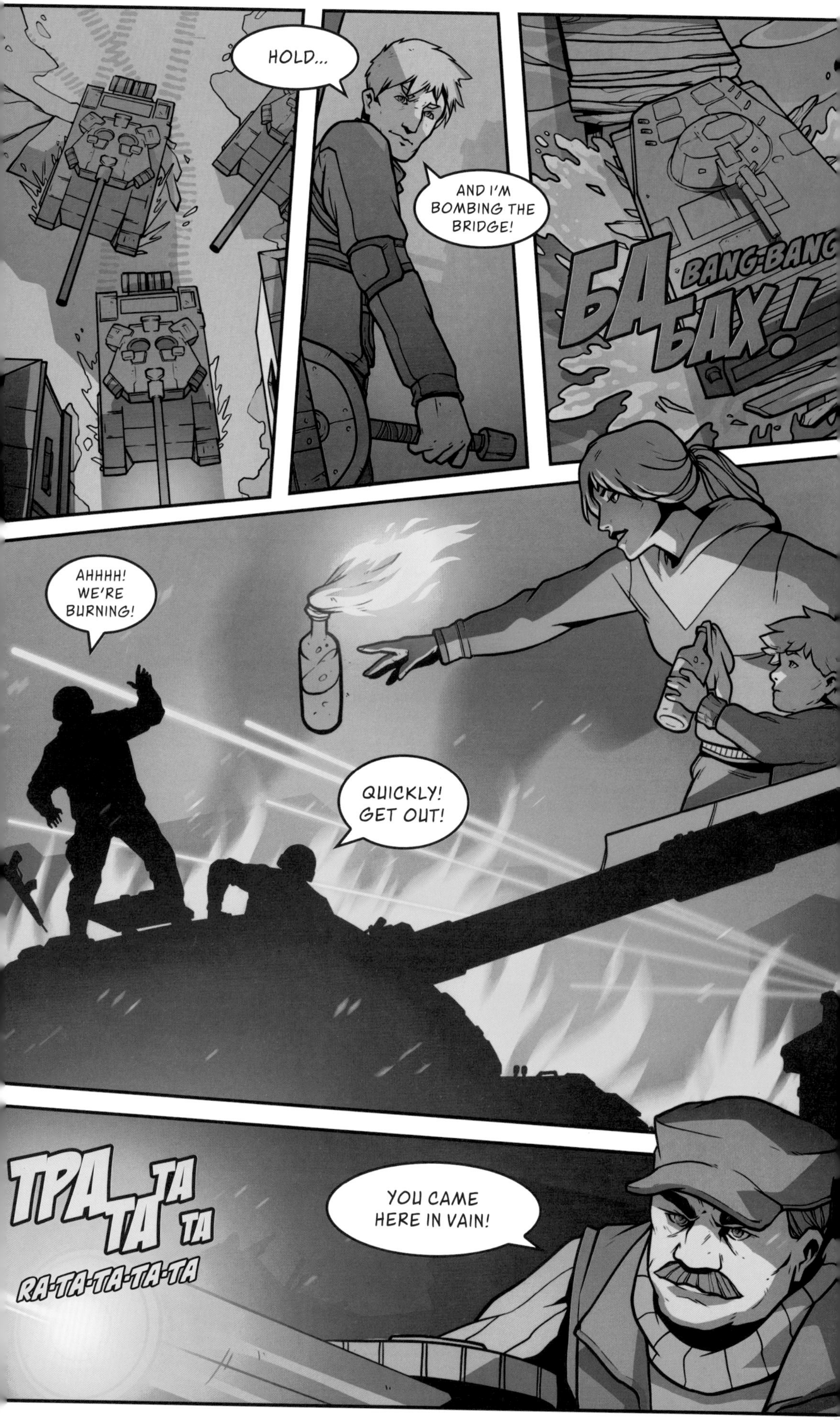
HOLD...
AND I'M BOMBING THE BRIDGE!
БА БАХ!
BANG-BANG
AHHHH! WE'RE BURNING!
QUICKLY! GET OUT!
ТРА ТА ТА ТА
RA-TA-TA-TA-TA
YOU CAME HERE IN VAIN!

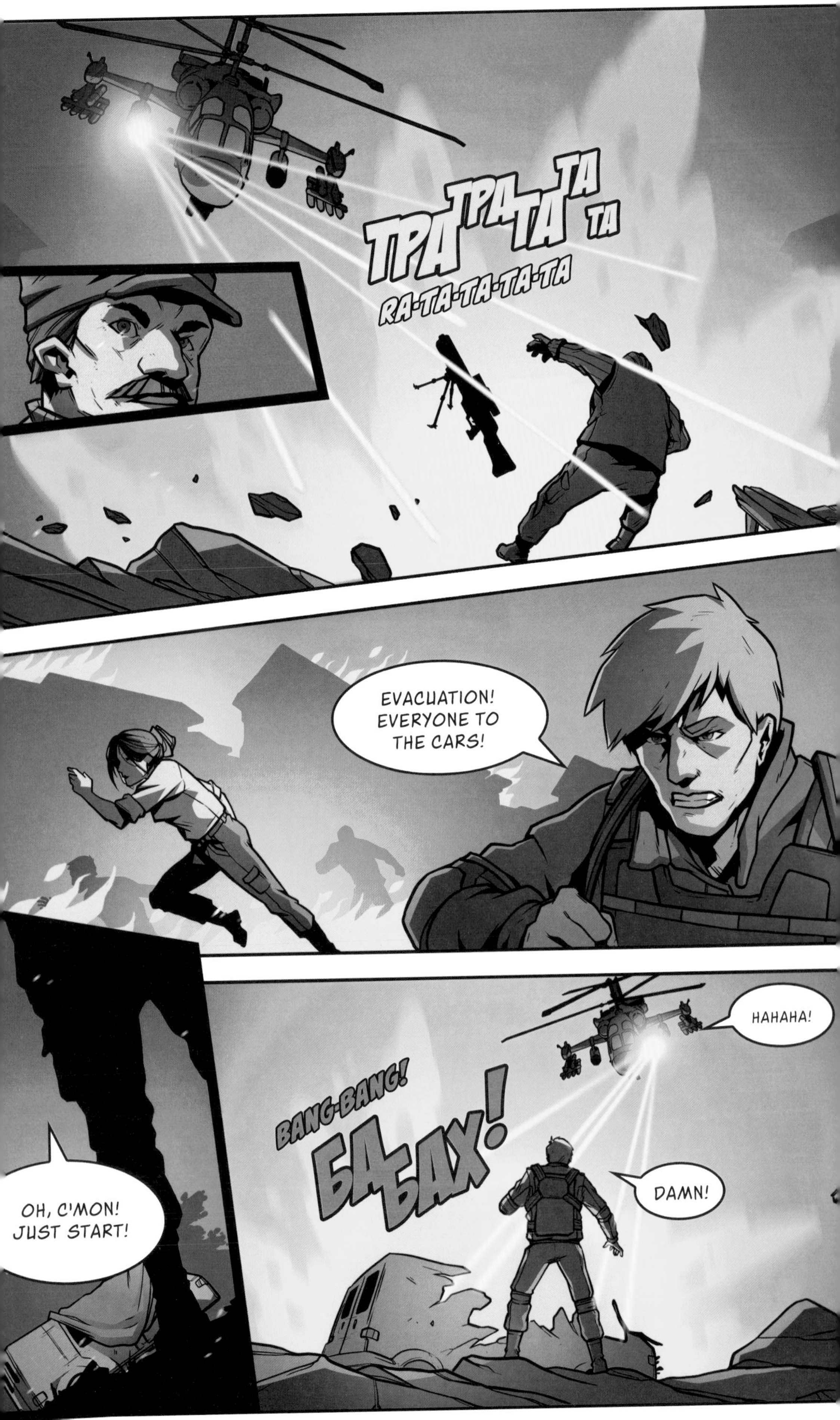
ТРА ТРА ТА ТА ТА
RA-TA-TA-TA-TA
EVACUATION! EVERYONE TO THE CARS!
HAHAHA!
BANG-BANG!
БАБАХ!
DAMN!
OH, C'MON! JUST START!

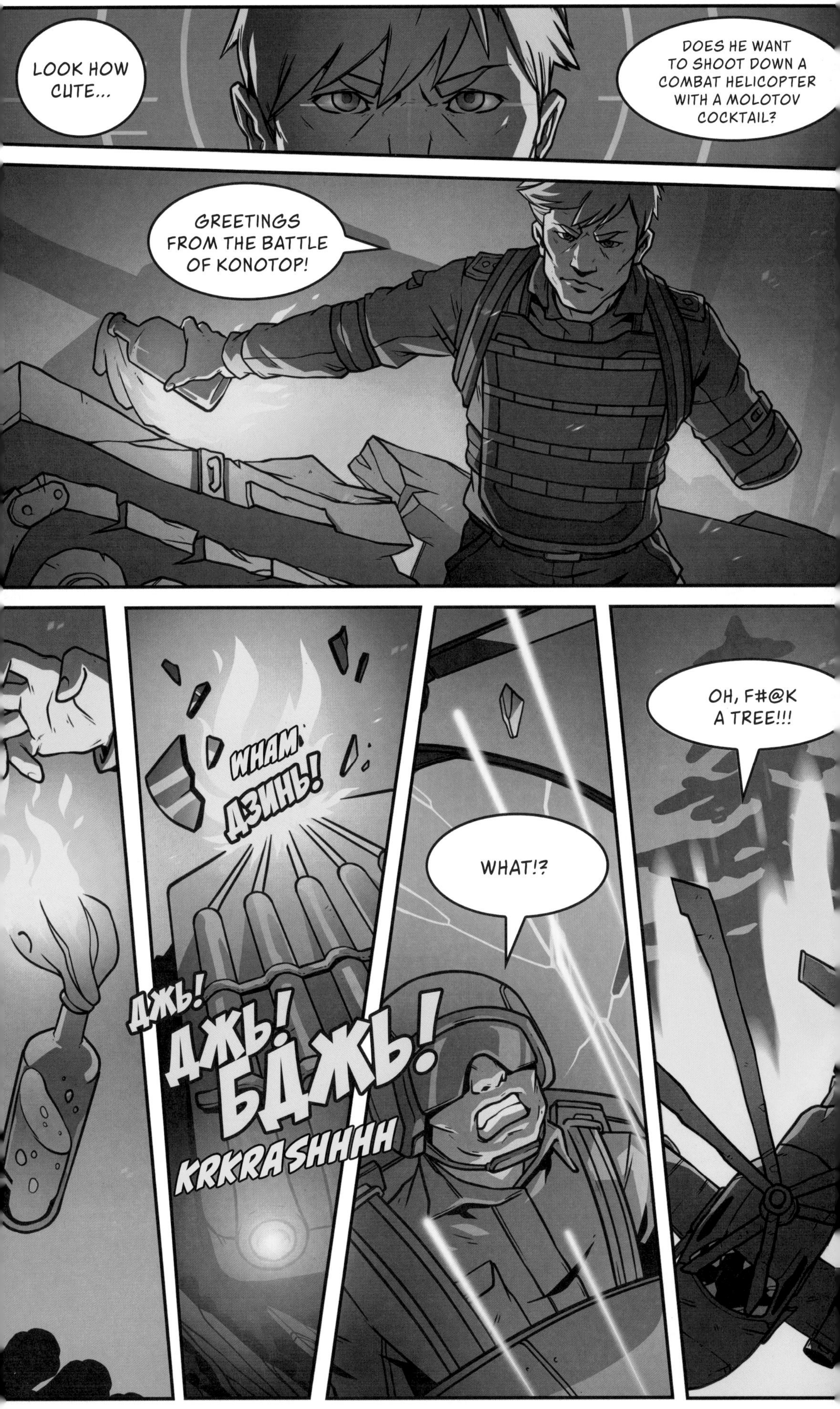
LOOK HOW CUTE...
DOES HE WANT TO SHOOT DOWN A COMBAT HELICOPTER WITH A MOLOTOV COCKTAIL?
GREETINGS FROM THE BATTLE OF KONOTOP!
WHAM
ДЗИНЬ!
ДЖЬ!
ДЖЬ!
БДЖЬ!
KRKRASHHHH
WHAT!?
OH, F#@K A TREE!!!

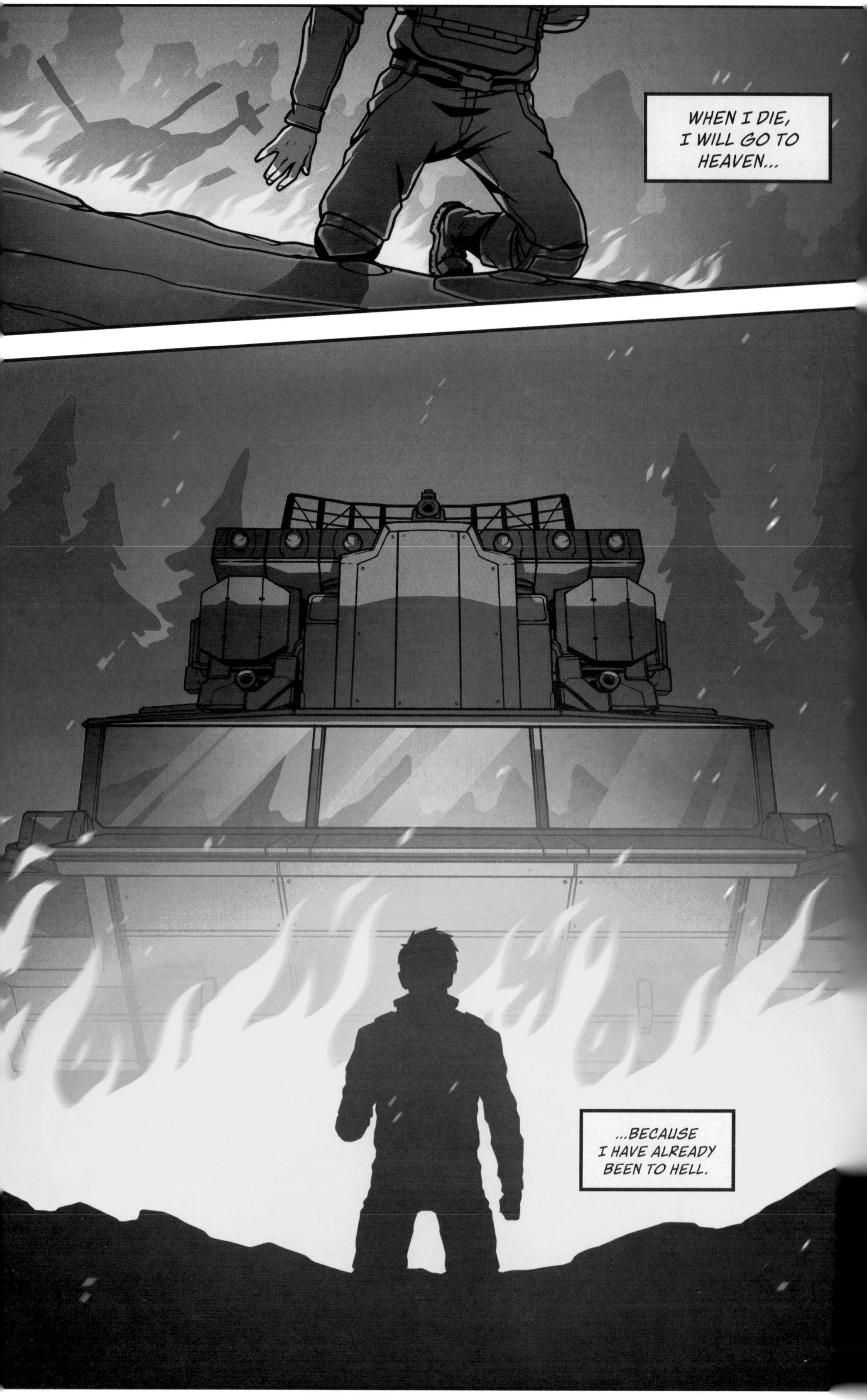
WHEN I DIE, I WILL GO TO HEAVEN...
...BECAUSE I HAVE ALREADY BEEN TO HELL.

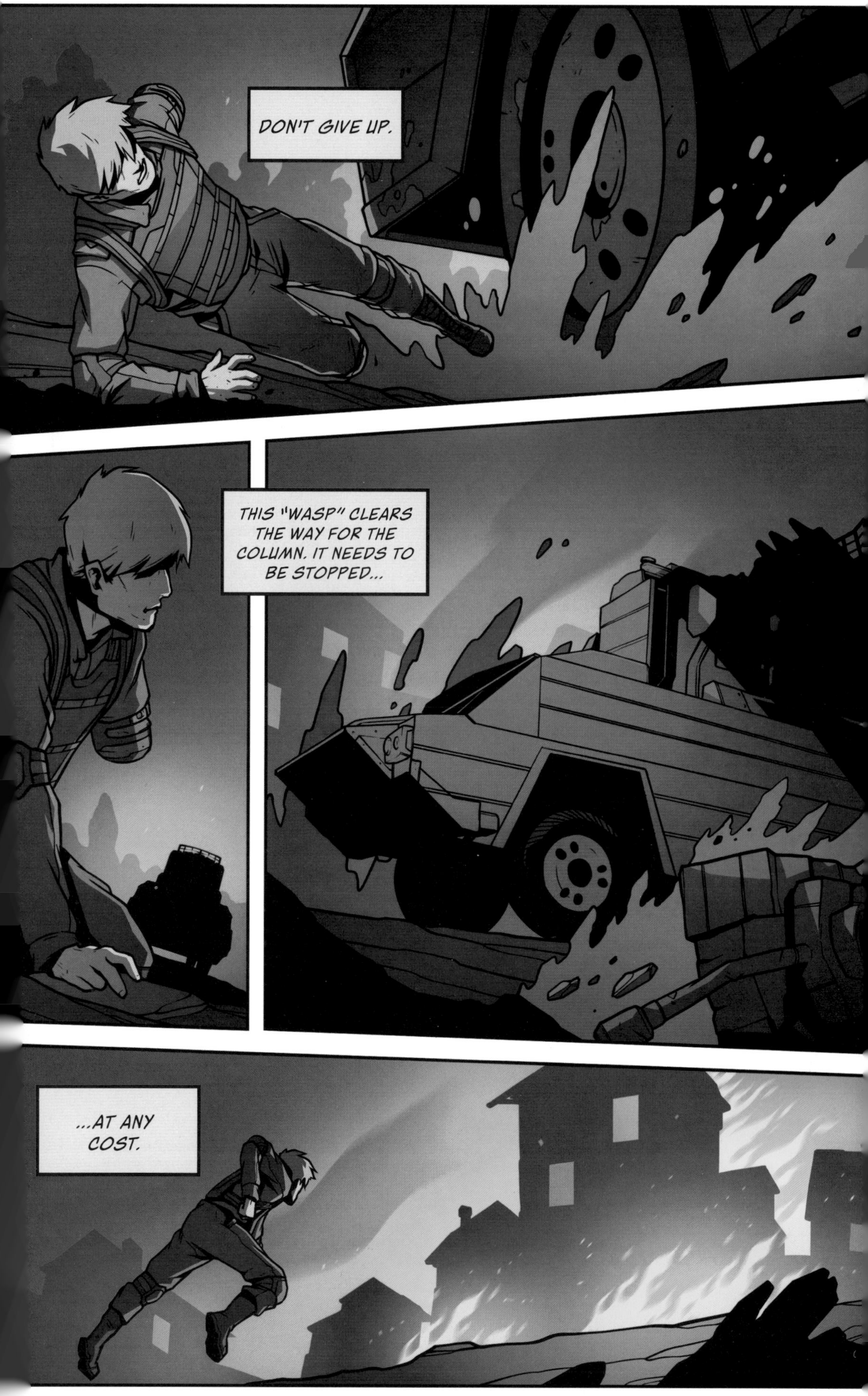
DON'T GIVE UP.
THIS "WASP" CLEARS THE WAY FOR THE COLUMN. IT NEEDS TO BE STOPPED...
...AT ANY COST.

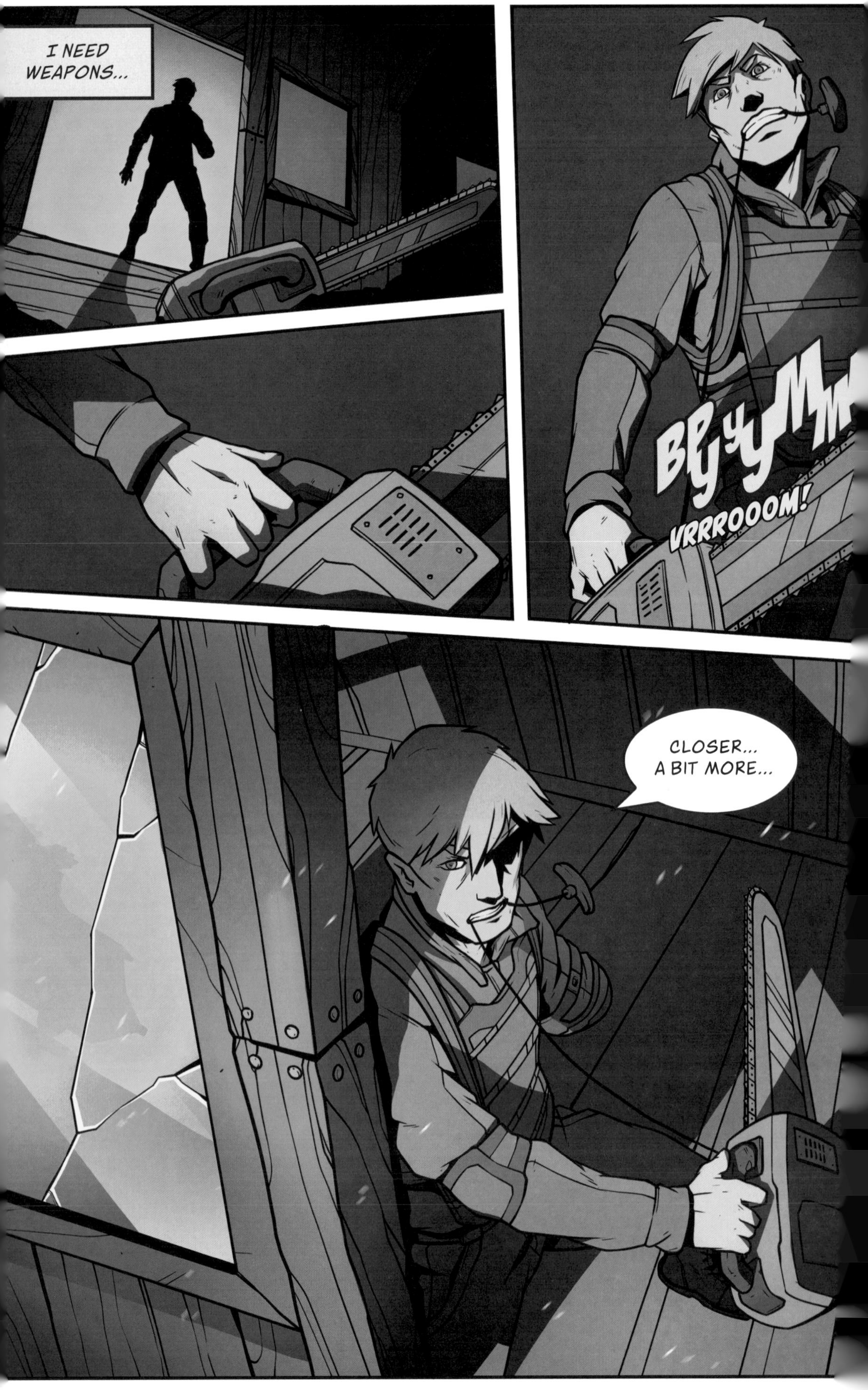
I NEED WEAPONS...
VRRROOOM!
CLOSER... A BIT MORE...

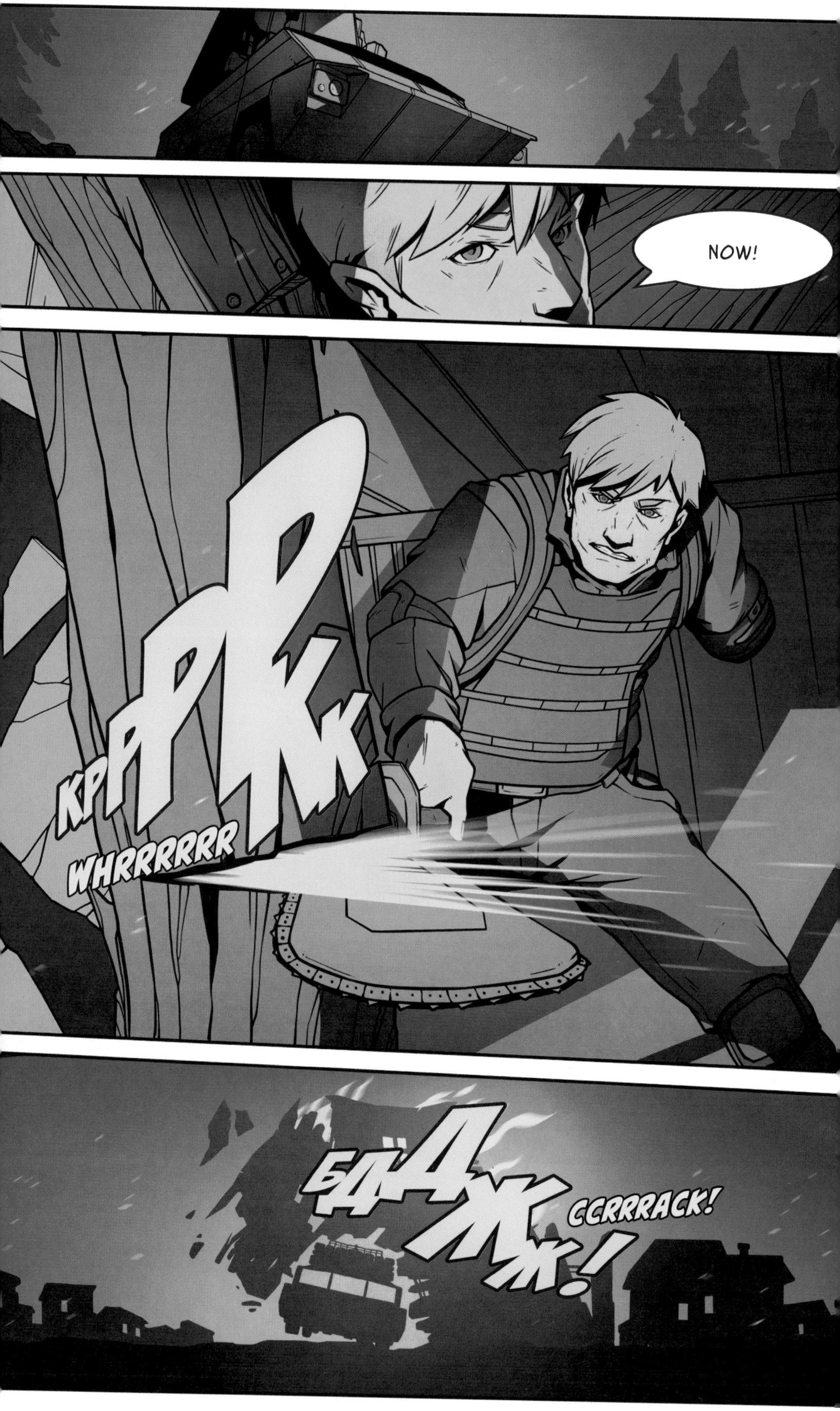
NOW!
КРРРк
WHRRRRRR
БДДЖж!
CCRRRACK!

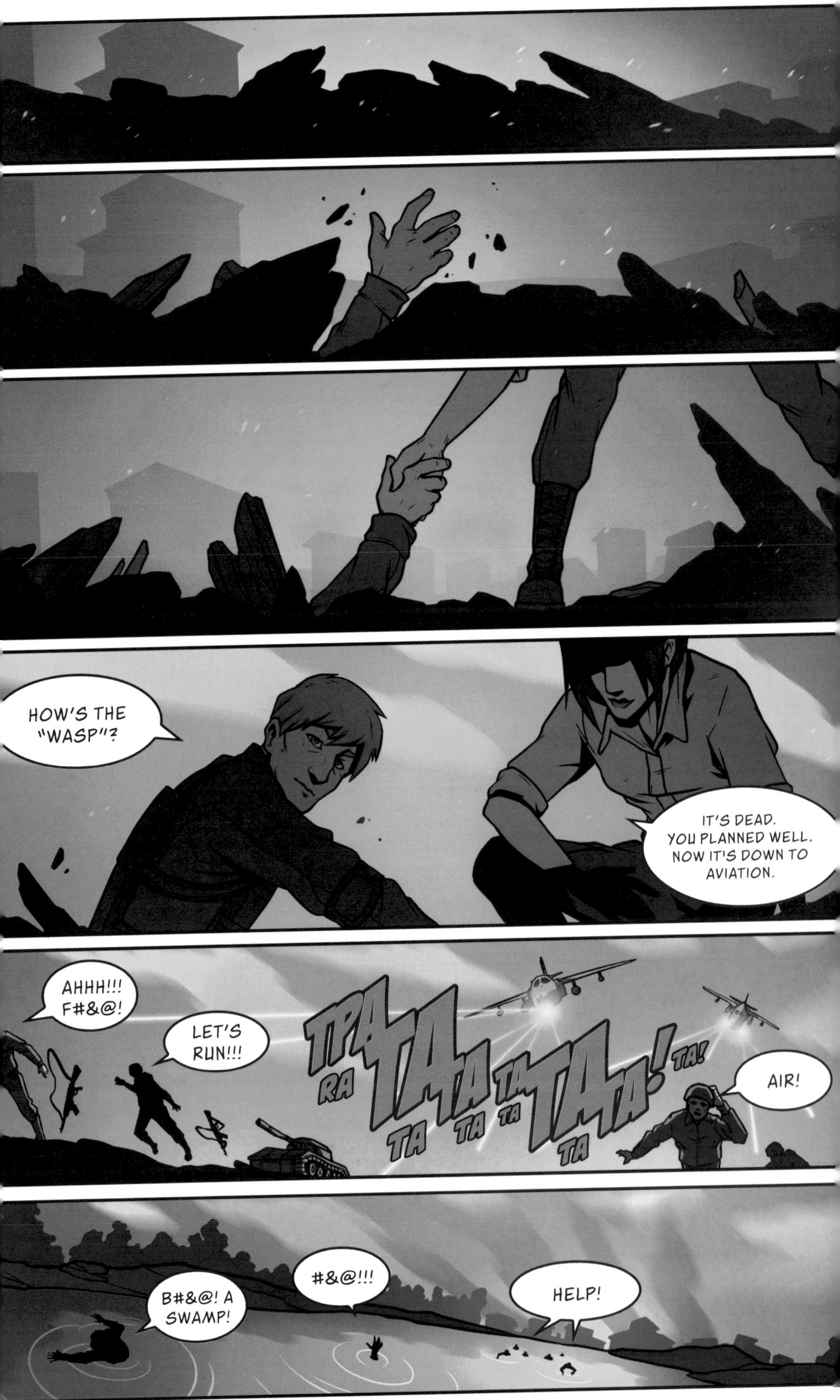
HOW'S THE "WASP"?
IT'S DEAD. YOU PLANNED WELL. NOW IT'S DOWN TO AVIATION.
AHHH!!! F#&@!
LET'S RUN!!!
TPA RA TA TA TA TA TA TA TA TA TA TA! TA!
AIR!
B#&@! A SWAMP!
#&@!!!
HELP!

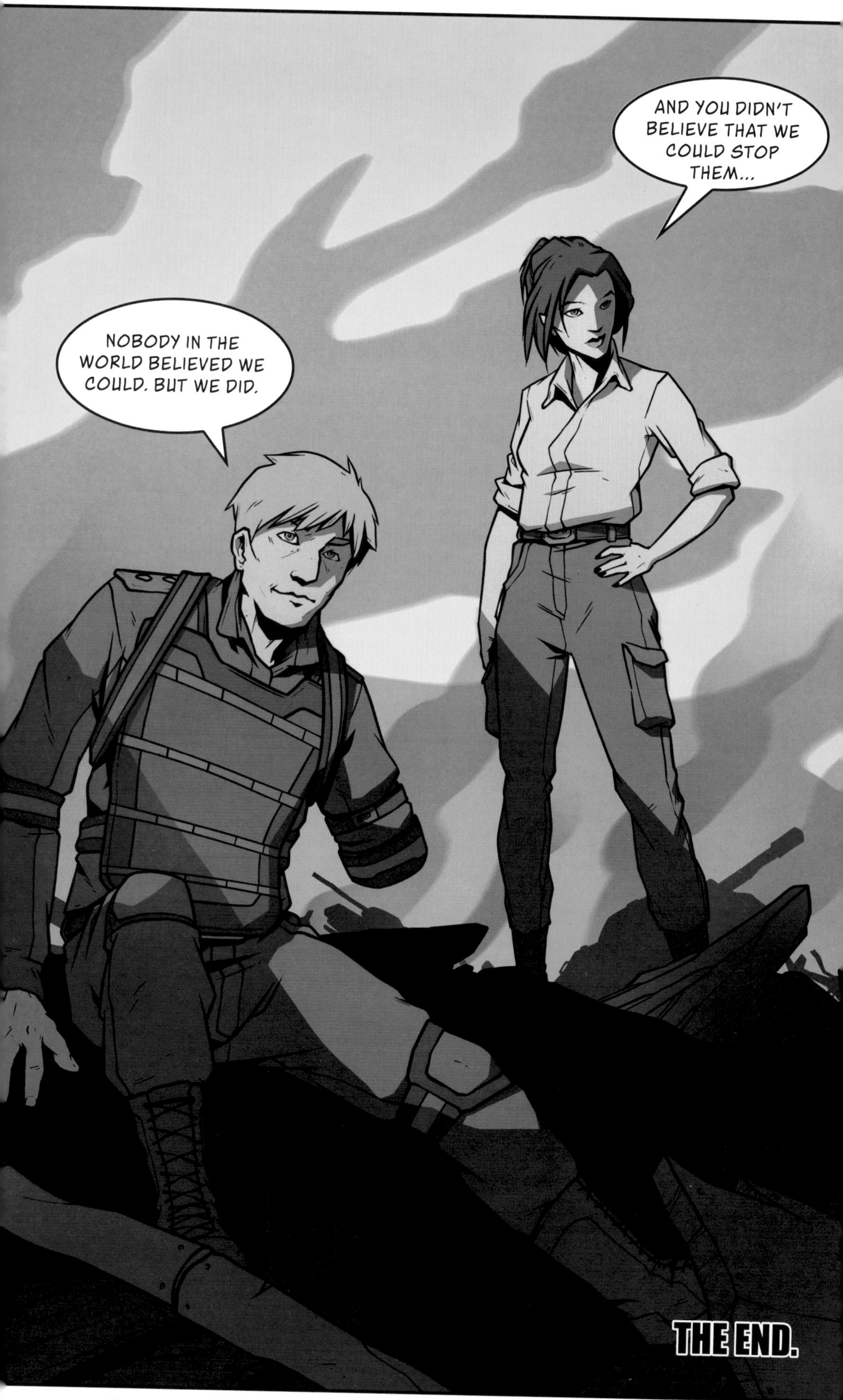
AND YOU DIDN'T BELIEVE THAT WE COULD STOP THEM...
NOBODY IN THE WORLD BELIEVED WE COULD. BUT WE DID.
THE END.

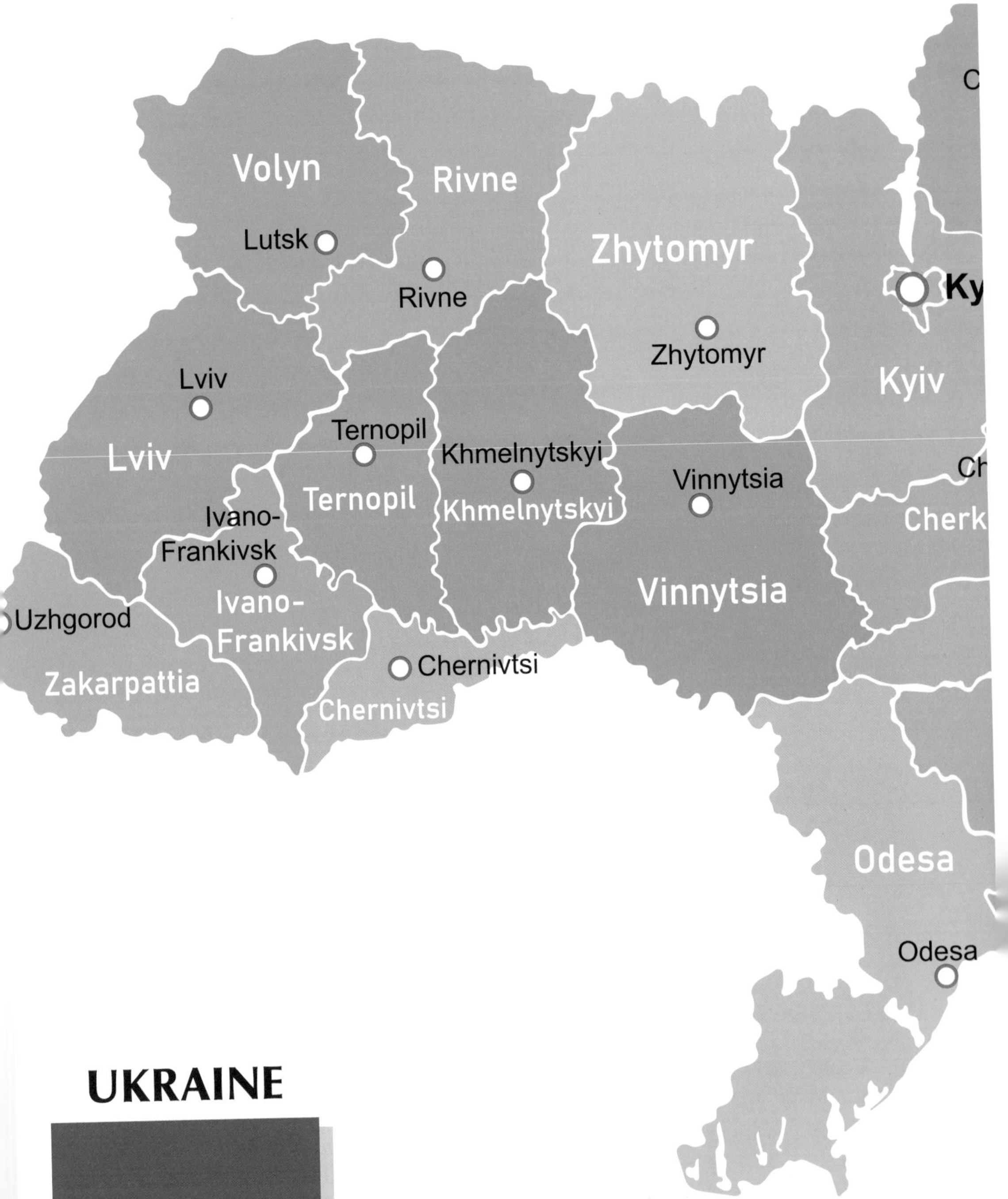
Volyn
Lutsk
Rivne
Rivne
Zhytomyr
Zhytomyr
Kyiv
Lviv
Lviv
Ternopil
Ternopil
Khmelnytskyi
Khmelnytskyi
Vinnytsia
Vinnytsia
Ivano-Frankivsk
Ivano-Frankivsk
Uzhgorod
Zakarpattia
Chernivtsi
Chernivtsi
Odesa
Odesa

UKRAINE

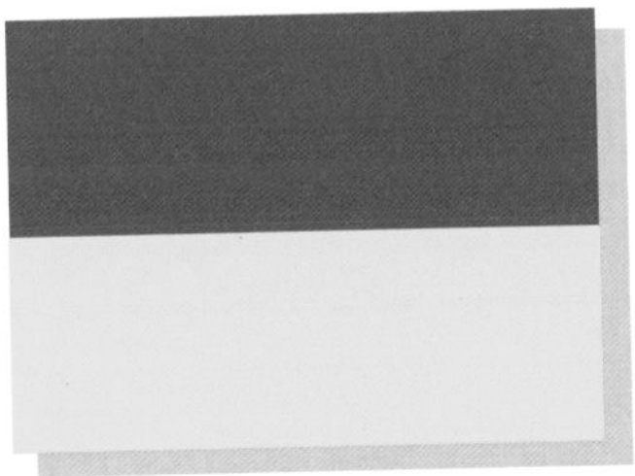

Chernihiv

Chernihiv

Sumy

Sumy

iv

Poltava

Kharkiv

Kharkiv

erkasy

asy

Poltava

Kropyvnytskyi

Dnipro

Luhansk

Kirovohrad

Dnipropetrovsk

Donetsk

Luhansk

Mykolaiv

Zaporizhzhia

Donetsk

Mykolaiv

Zaporizhzhia

Kherson

Crimea

Simferopol

Sevastopol

Eduard Akhramovych
General Producer

I'm a producer, so I'm involved not only in the production of comics, but also in the production of animated cartoons. I headed the legendary Ukrainian studio "Ukranimafilm" for many years. I produced anime series, full-length and short animated films. They are available on Youtube (the name of the channel is ukranimaua) and gather millions of views both in Ukraine and abroad.

My family and I have experienced a lot of terrible moments since the first days of aggressive Russian occupation, including the shelling of residential areas by Russian artillery. I had to evacuate my family to the west part of the country so that they would be safer and less at risk during the numerous air alarms. I was forced to put my business on hold and close our office. In May, I gradually started to return my employees to the office so the creative team could support the valiant heroes of our army in the eastern part of our country with our projects.

My personal slogan is "Create where you are"! And because of this, we continue to create new works even during this time of war. So I ask American readers to not forget our struggle against the dark forces from the past centuries.

Denys Fadieiev
Writer, Episodes 1, 2, 3, 5, 6, 8, 9

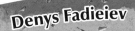

The first full-format comic I created was in 2015. It's called "Battle for Ukraine" (in Ukrainian: "Zvityaga. Savur Mogyla"), and it's available on Amazon. Thanks to that comic, I met the wonderful V'yacheslav Bugayovych and Oleksandr Filipovych, and together we created The Will Production in 2017. Our comics are read all over the world now. Our irreplaceable manager and historical consultant Olga Vozniuk joined our team later, when we were no longer able to process the huge number of requests because The Will became a national bestseller.

From the moment I woke up to the sound of explosions at 5:00 a.m. on the 24th of February, I had thousands of reasons to find inspiration. The information flow about the heroism and intelligence of Ukrainian soldiers was off the scale—like the story about defenders of Zmiinyi Island who set the trend from the first day of occupation and created the meme that will live forever: "Russian warship—go f*** yourself!"

Support Ukraine. Take care of our refugees. Even a few dollars can break the spine of the Russian monster.

Viacheslav Buhaiov

Project Leader

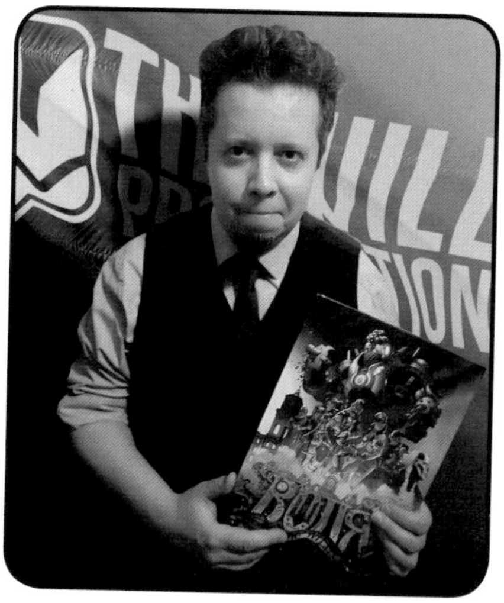

This war divided my family off to different countries of Europe. We had a very hard, stressful situation during the first month. But I was able to recover my emotions soon and follow them into a new project—"Перемога: Victory for Ukraine". It is going to help our country and the army. We are also doing a lot as volunteers to buy ammunition for the troops.

This comic is about real, genuine emotions of its artists and writers—all people who created it under dangerous circumstances. It is the cry of the souls of the Ukrainian people. A cry of anger and pain, but at the same time it is a cry of love for our motherland and a cry for victory, which will definitely happen.

I would like to also address a message to foreign readers. Please never think of any war in the world as one that bypasses you. It is the biggest mistake in the world that makes war happen again and again. The atrocities Russia has committed since the beginning of its existence—Abkhazia, Chechnya, Moldova, Ossetia, Syria, Ukraine—are examples of violence and war crimes that the world closes their eyes to in the hope of avoiding a war with a nuclear country. But this has led to Russia being ready to drown not only Ukraine but all Europe in blood.

Oleksandr Koreshkov

Artist, Episode 1 - The Ghost of Kyiv

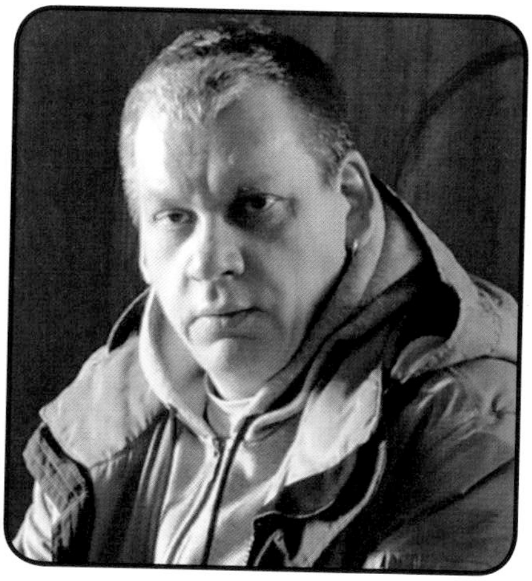

This war has been going on for a long time. At least since 2014. On the 24th of February 2022, I woke up at around 5 a.m. because the glass panes of my windows were shaking. I called everyone I knew and told them that the invasion had begun (if they didn't know already). It was scary listening to all-day bombings. After a month, my brother went to Mykolayiv to pick up my wife and our mother. And it was one of the most important decisions in my life. Now they are safe.

The Ghost of Kyiv has been a legend since the first hours of the invasion by the Russians. In one day, he shot down 6 (six!) enemy airplanes. He is a real superhero! And when I was offered topics to choose from, I did not hesitate. I took the story of Ghost of Kyiv. Only I had the courage to adapt it to 10 pages. I have also been a fan of airplanes since my childhood ☺

I would like to talk about the solidarity of the civilized world and so on, but it is more important to pass the following message: JUST BELIEVE Ukraine and take ALL that comes from Russia as absolute nonsense. They are the anti-Midas: everything they touch turns to sh**, pain, and death.

Kateryna Kosheleva

Artist, Episode 2 - The Witch

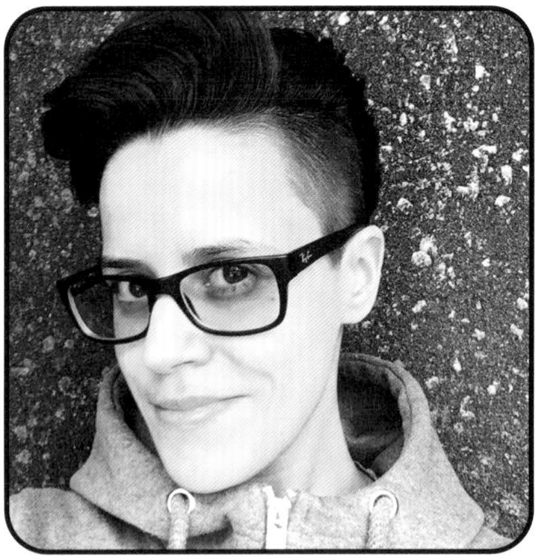

"The Witch" was inspired by my home region of Sumy and the town of Konotop in particular. There is this half-joking notion that every other woman there is a witch (probably in greater part stemming from the novel "The Witch of Konotop" by Kvitka-Osnovianenko). And hearing the stories, watching the news, I thought that maybe this war has awakened something in my people, something ancient and fundamental, something better not be trifled with. I made a sketch trying to capture this raw force, a delicate woman dismantling a tank, and I was amazed when Denys Fadieev managed to turn that illustration into a script that captured the essence of that story of resistance so perfectly.

The past several years have demonstrated how fragile our civilization is. What is happening now in Ukraine has global significance because, right at this moment, men and women with Ukrainian flags on their uniforms fight to shield and preserve civilization. The harsh truth is that this war is a model of things to come: civilization versus barbarians, truth versus lies, integrity versus corruption, with little place for moral relativism. There is no doubt in my mind that "the things good and proper" will prevail eventually, and I hope each and every one of us will have played our part, no matter how small, in making that Victory possible. My heartfelt thanks go to those who help and support Ukraine. Thank you!

Ihor Kurilin

Artist, Episode 5 - Zmiinyi Island 13

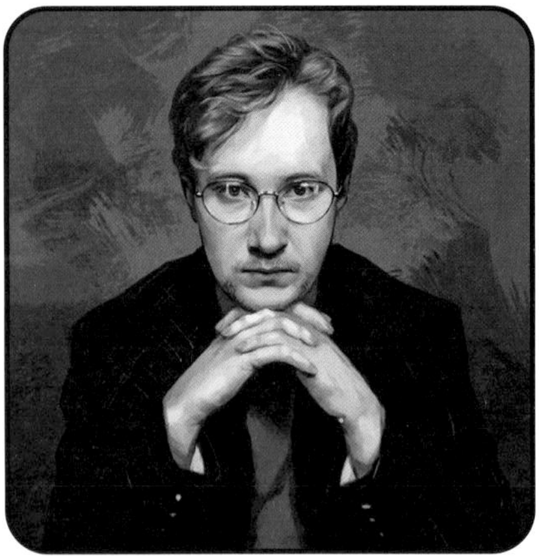

The war strongly influenced my relationship with many things. I began to value and to admire Ukrainian content even more than before and I saw how rich our culture is with talented people. I began to listen to more Ukrainian songs, to read Ukrainian literature, and to study Ukrainian history. I fully gave up any Russian content on the internet.

I really like the story I created about Zmiiniy Island because it's based on real events that took place at the beginning of the war. This story became a legend among Ukrainians. And it's about the courage of our troops, which is why I am proud to be a part of this story. It's a story about how, even in face of any threat, it is necessary to be calm and to believe that truth will always be victorious in the world.

Kyrylo (Kir) Malov

Artist, Episode 9 - The Price of Victory

My family and I had to move from Kyiv, and, despite how big that is, I think the most important thing that changed for me is the fact that I decided to not delay anything in my life that is possible to not delay, and my loved ones also share this philosophy now. I realized it while standing near my house on February 24 at 6 a.m., listening to the first air raid sirens and first explosions. You never know what will happen, so if you want to do something, say something, learn something, create something you were always thinking of—do it today, not tomorrow, not in a month.

Art has always been my main job, and I've worked as a concept artist, illustrator and comics artist in different fields like game development, movie and TV production. As I was only an illustrator of this story ["The Price of Victory"], I still wanted to add something personal. And in this particular project, it was a feeling of hope and how, through rage and bravery, we are still heading to the sunset at the end of this long night.

My dream is pretty simple these days. As I recommend to our readers, I want to stop hesitating, do something big, and share something beautiful with people through art, music, cinema etc. I'm still curious about what exactly it will be.

Please support Ukraine and our struggle for freedom.

Nazar Ponik
Artist, Episode 8 - Cyber-Kherson

I've worked as a 2D-artist and developed video game graphics as well as created art for computer and mobile games. Since 2022, I have been working as Senior 2D-artist in the Ukrainian company Stepico Games. I also work as a freelancer, drawing and coloring comics at The Will Productions. Since my early childhood I've loved drawing and did it so often that later on, despite my degree in another field, I returned to my passion.

I've drawn this story because, for me, a particularly sensitive situation happened in the city of Kherson, which has suffered from Russian occupation since the early weeks of war. There, local people flooded the streets and shouted "Kherson is Ukraine!" And I cannot wait till this city becomes free again!

I would like to tell the readers this: do not forget that there's still war raging in Ukraine, and we need your help by any means possible. Talk about it, write about it.

Bohdana (Dana) Vitkovska
Artist, Episode 7 - Brave Little Tractor

I grew up in a family of Ukrainian Roman Catholics—my great grandparents were Polish, but I was raised in the atmosphere of patriotism and love towards my homeland of Ukraine. I am and I feel fully Ukrainian. Soon after my graduation from university, I realized that I couldn't live without doing art on a daily basis, so I decided to pursue the career of an artist. And it is a decision I've never regretted. Four years ago, I moved to Kyiv and have been living there since then. Firstly, it was quite difficult to get used to such a big and unfamiliar city. I was mad about the noise, crowds, and long commutes. But I realized my deep feelings toward this city when the War began—with the threat of it being occupied or destroyed. As for my future, I would not like to leave my country. I want to stay in Ukraine and help her get back on her feet after the war. Here is my home, and I am an integral part of it.

The first hours of the war were hard. But somewhere inside I always knew it would happen, so the state of shock faded away soon. We (me and my fiancée) were determined to stay and protect our city and country. We don't have any military experience, so the Army doesn't need us yet. But we are ready to fight when it's our turn. When war comes, your plans for your life don't mean anything anymore. We were planning to have our wedding in the spring but had to postpone it. We are still unsure if it's ethical to celebrate a wedding when so much pain and horror is happening to our people. But things are getting better now, at least for me. I couldn't listen to music, watch movies, or allow myself to do anything that reminded me of the joyful pre-war time at first. Now I try to take my joy for life back, gradually. And I hope more and more Ukrainians will be able to do that soon.

TOKYOPOP
supports
Ukraine,
and you can
too...

A portion of
proceeds from this book
will be donated to the charity
RAZOM (which means "together"
in Ukrainian). RAZOM is a non-
profit Ukrainian-American human
rights organization established to
give direct support to the people
of Ukraine in their pursuit of a
democratic society with dignity,
justice, and human and
civil rights for all.

RAZO
RazomForUkraine